W9-AXO-691

MAJESTIC EXPRESSIONS

Relax. Refresh. Renew

New Every Morning

INSPIRATIONAL ADULT COLORING BOOK

BroadStreet
PUBLISHING

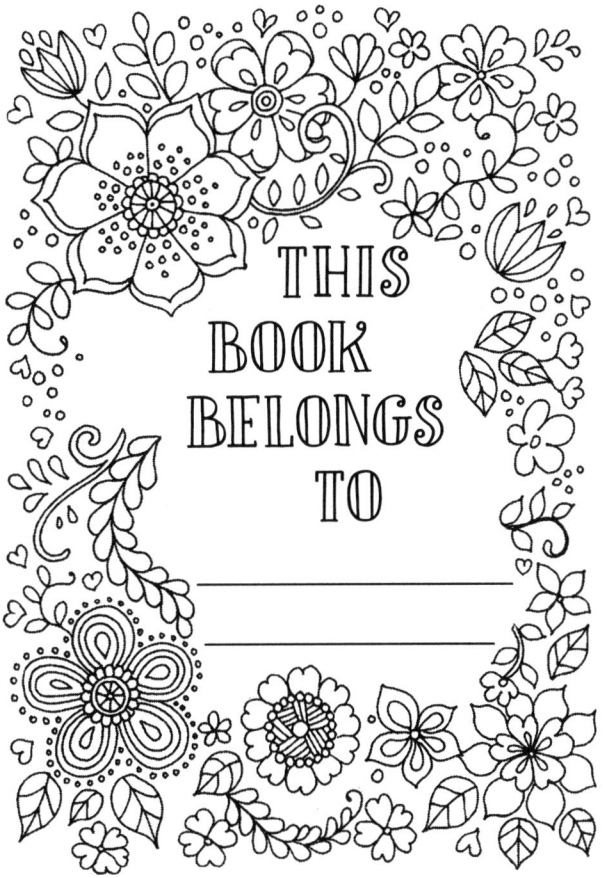
THIS
BOOK
BELONGS
TO

BroadStreet Publishing Group LLC
Racine, Wisconsin, USA
Broadstreetpublishing.com

MAJESTIC EXPRESSIONS

NEW EVERY MORNING

© 2016 by BroadStreet Publishing

ISBN 978-1-4245-4924-5

All rights reserved. No part of this publication may be reproduced, distributed, or transmitted in any form or by any means, including photocopying, recording, or other electronic or mechanical methods, without the prior written permission of the publisher, except in the case of brief quotations embodied in critical reviews and certain other noncommercial uses permitted by copyright law.

Scripture quotations marked (NLT) are taken from the Holy Bible, New Living Translation, copyright © 1996, 2004, 2007. Used by permission of Tyndale House Publishers, Inc., Carol Stream, Illinois 60188. All rights reserved. Scripture quotations marked (NIV) are taken from the Holy Bible, New International Version®, NIV®. Copyright © 1973, 1978, 1984, 2011 by Biblica, Inc.™ Used by permission of Zondervan. All rights reserved worldwide. www.zondervan.com. The "NIV" and "New International Version" are trademarks registered in the United States Patent and Trademark Office by Biblica, Inc.™ Scripture quotations marked (NCV) are taken from the New Century Version®. Copyright © 2005 by Thomas Nelson. Used by permission. Scripture quotations marked (NASB) are taken from the New American Standard Bible®, Copyright © 1960, 1962, 1963, 1968, 1971, 1972, 1973, 1975, 1977, 1995 by The Lockman Foundation. Used by permission. www.Lockman.org. Scripture quotations marked (NRSV) are taken from the New Revised Standard Version Bible, copyright 1989, Division of Christian Education of the National Council of the Churches of Christ in the United States of America. Used by permission. All rights reserved. Scripture quotations marked (ESV) are from the ESV® Bible (The Holy Bible, English Standard Version®), copyright © 2001 by Crossway, a publishing ministry of Good News Publishers. Used by permission. All rights reserved. Scripture quotations marked HCSB®, are taken from the Holman Christian Standard Bible®, Copyright © 1999, 2000, 2002, 2003, 2009 by Holman Bible Publishers. Used by permission. HCSB® is a federally registered trademark of Holman Bible Publishers.

Cover design by Chris Garborg | garborgdesign.com
Compiled and edited by Michelle Winger | literallyprecise.com

Printed in the United States of America.

16 17 18 19 20 21 22 7 6 5 4 3 2 1

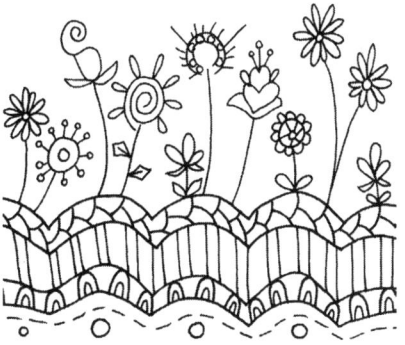

INTRODUCTION

There is plenty of research that shows coloring to be an effective stress reducer. Maybe you picked up this book because you've heard the hype and you're curious. Perhaps you've been looking for a way to relax. Now you have your very own adult coloring book, and you have every reason you need to sit down and color. And perforated pages make it easy for you to frame your favorites!

Coloring is a great distraction from all you have going on, but the best way to find lasting peace is to spend time with your Creator. Fill these intricately designed illustrations with the beauty of color as you dwell on the richness of his Word, the faithfulness of his character, and the depth of his love for you.

Happy coloring!

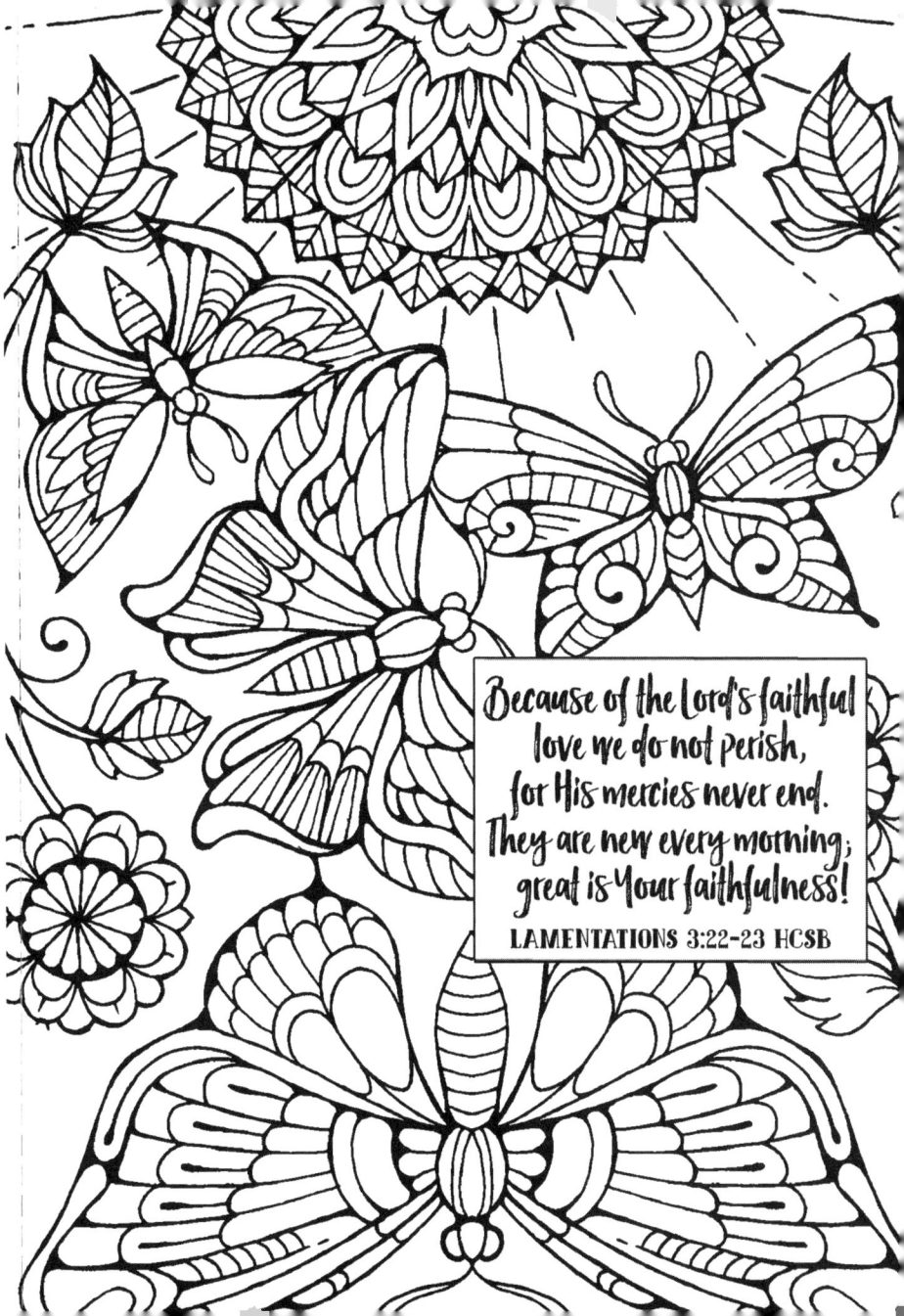
Because of the Lord's faithful
love we do not perish,
for His mercies never end.
They are new every morning;
great is Your faithfulness!
LAMENTATIONS 3:22-23 HCSB

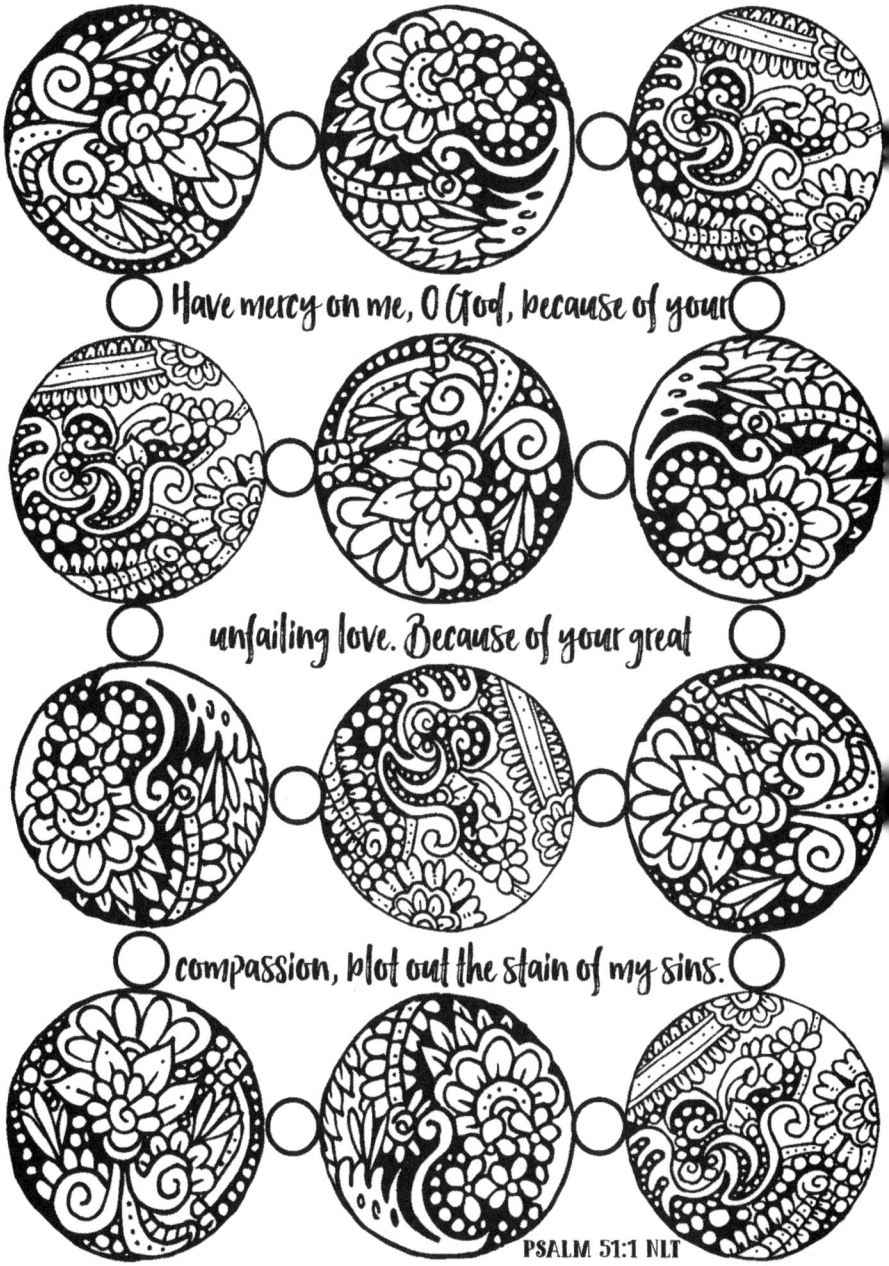
Have mercy on me, O God, because of your
unfailing love. Because of your great
compassion, blot out the stain of my sins.
PSALM 51:1 NLT

Keep alert,
stand firm in your faith, be courageous,
be strong. Let all that you do be done in love.

1 CORINTHIANS 16:13-14 NRSV

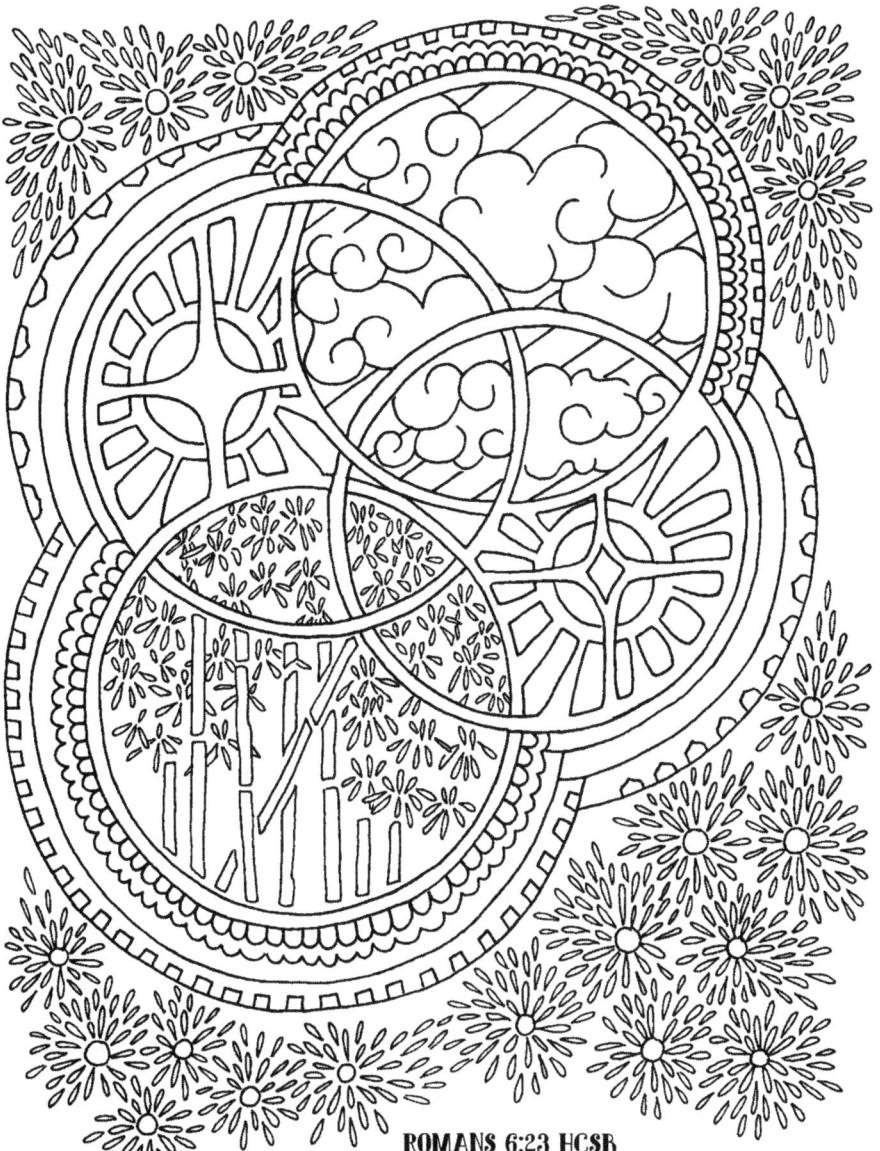

ROMANS 6:23 HCSB

For the wages of sin is death,
but the gift of God is eternal life in Christ Jesus our Lord.

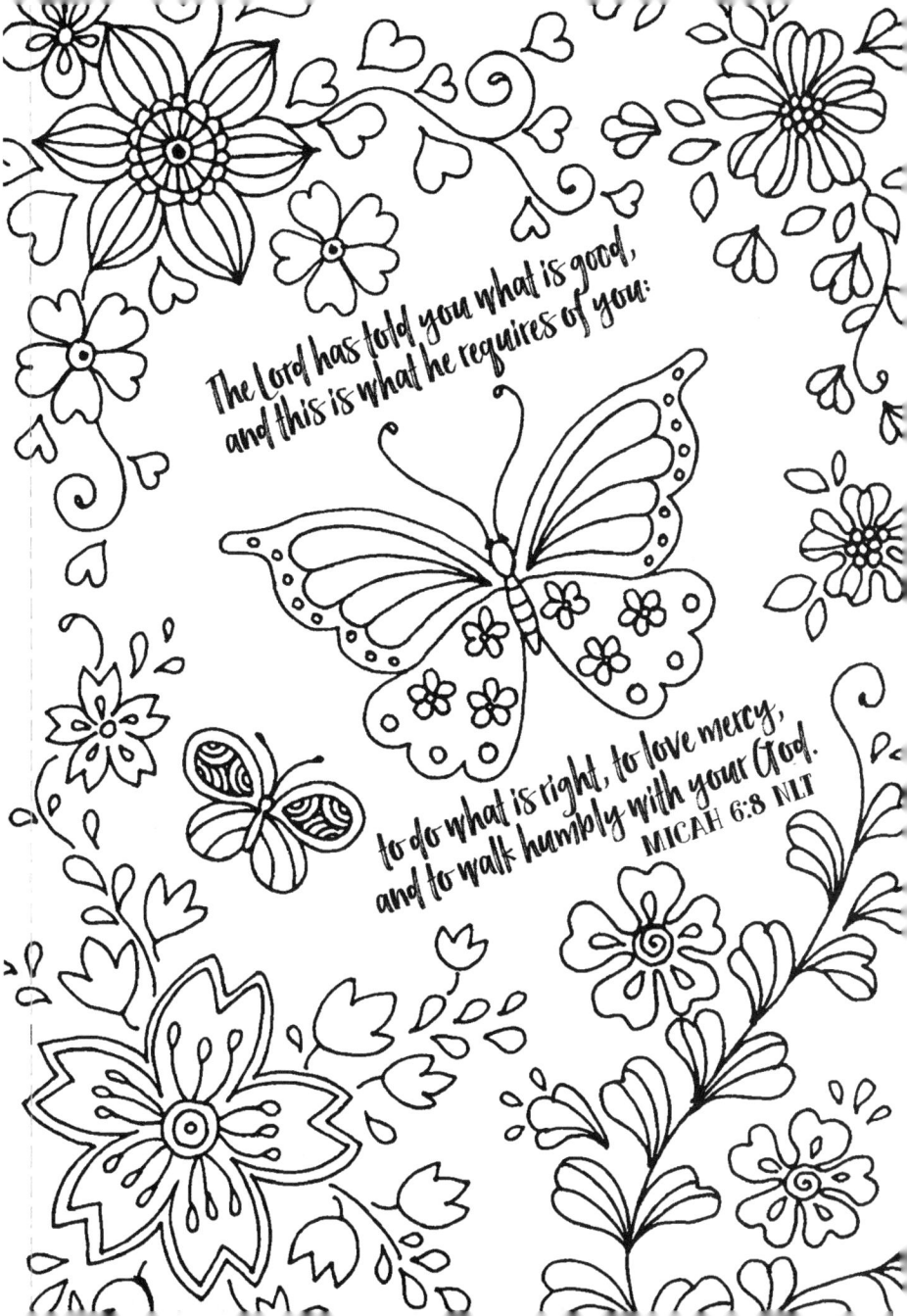
The Lord has told you what is good,
and this is what he requires of you:
to do what is right, to love mercy,
and to walk humbly with your God.
MICAH 6:8 NLT

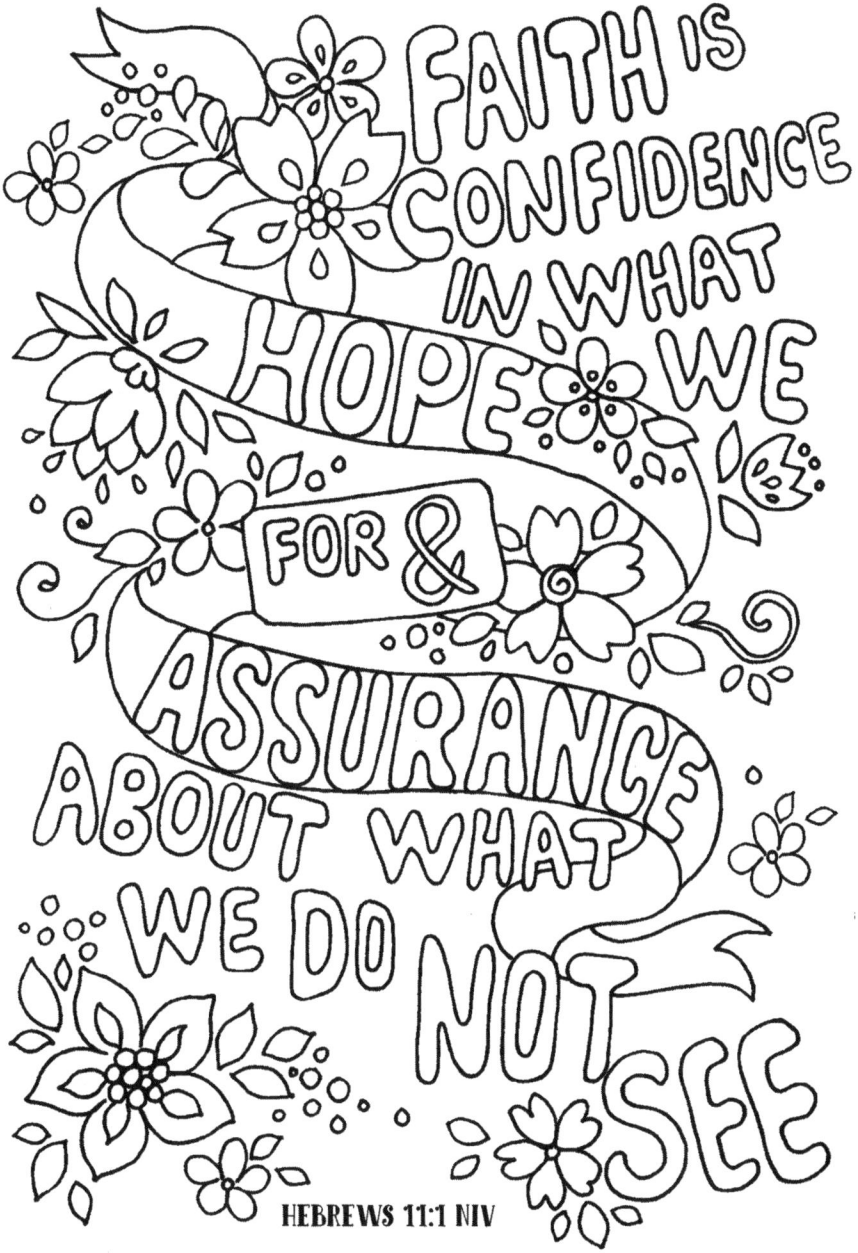
FAITH IS CONFIDENCE IN WHAT WE HOPE FOR & ASSURANCE ABOUT WHAT WE DO NOT SEE
HEBREWS 11:1 NIV

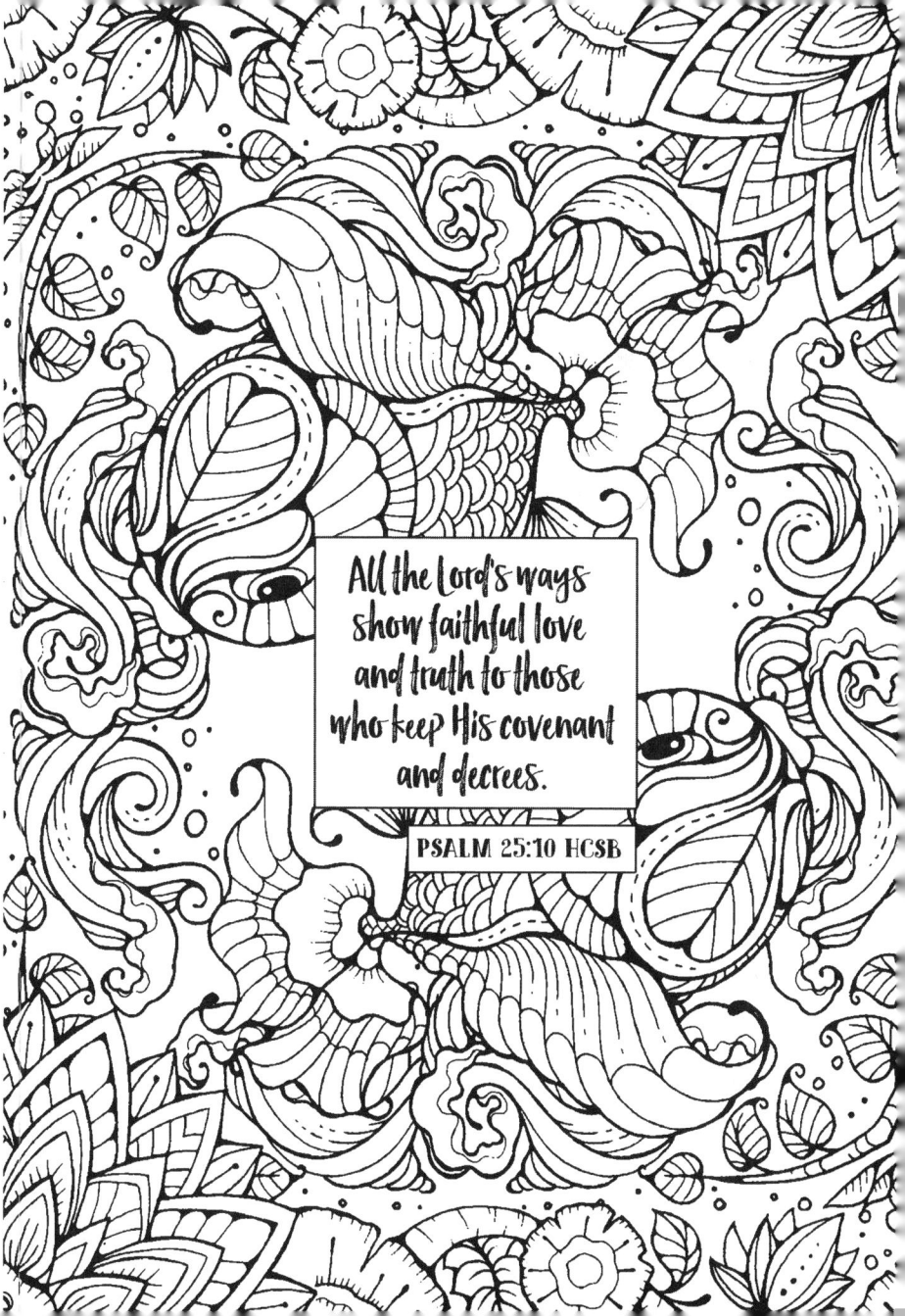
All the Lord's ways
show faithful love
and truth to those
who keep His covenant
and decrees.
PSALM 25:10 HCSB

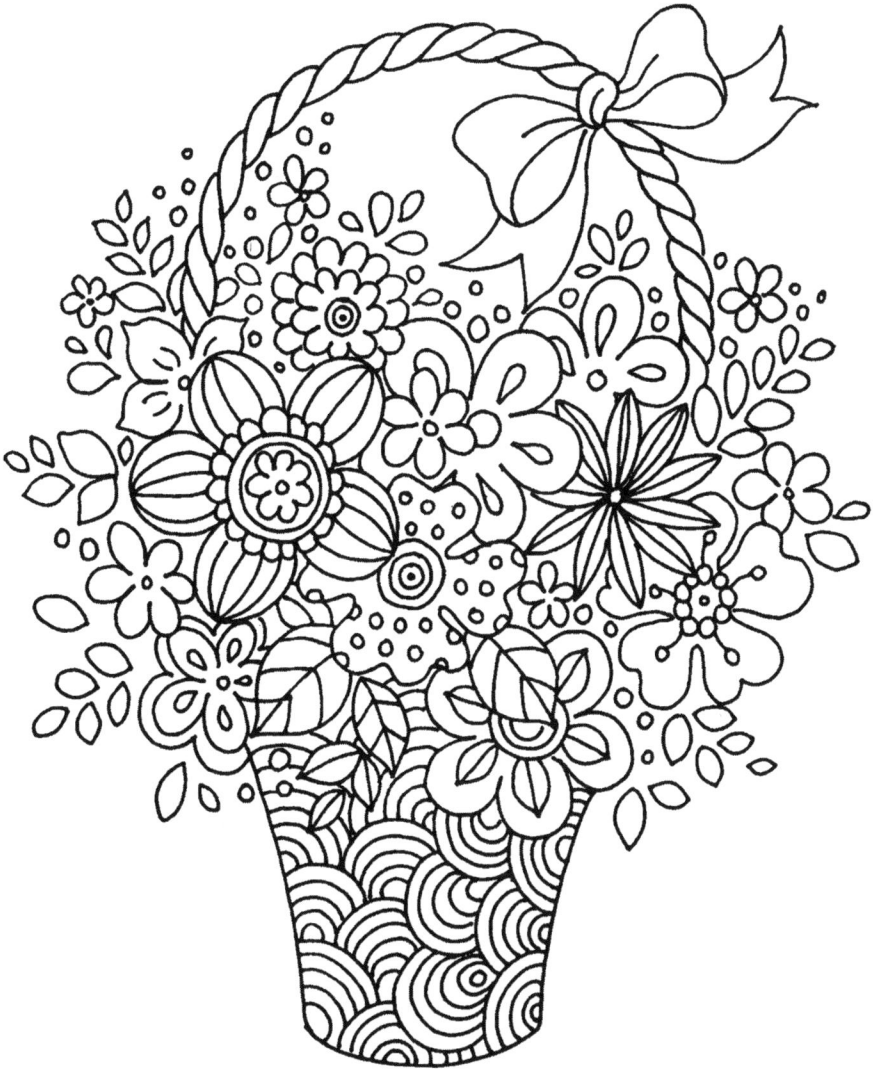

I will be faithful to you and make you mine,
and you will finally know me as the Lord.

HOSEA 2:20 NLT

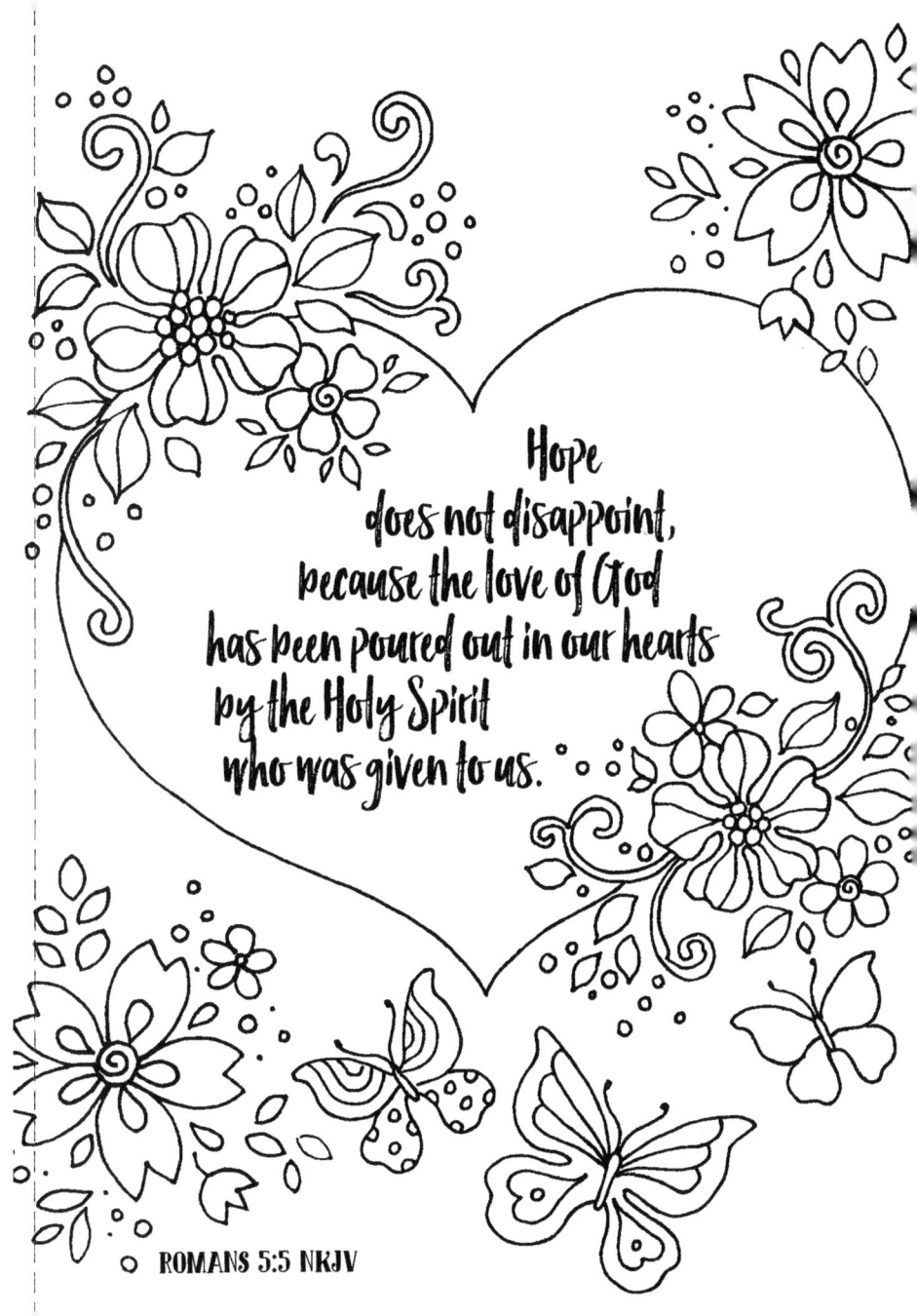
Hope
does not disappoint,
because the love of God
has been poured out in our hearts
by the Holy Spirit
who was given to us.
ROMANS 5:5 NKJV

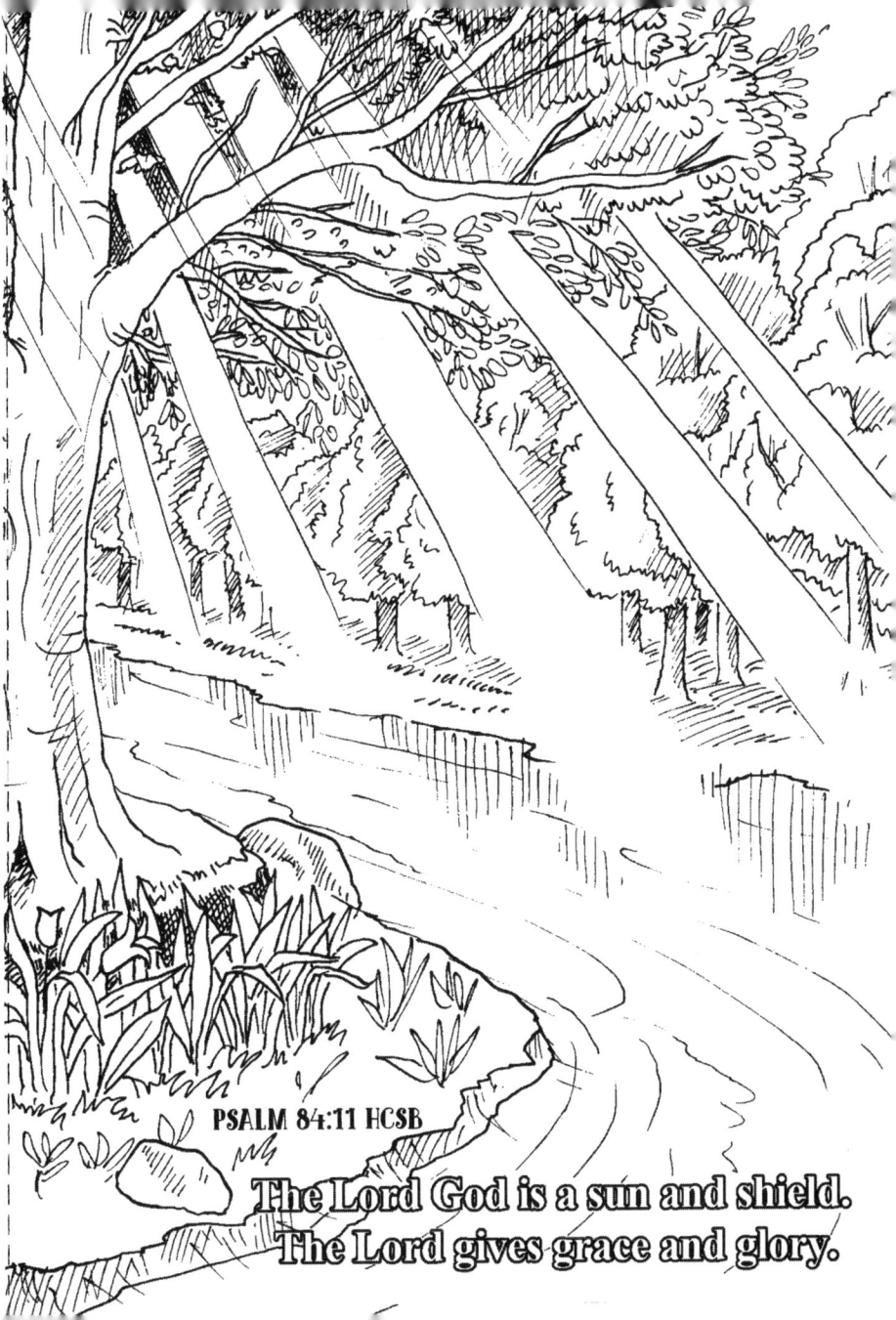
PSALM 84:11 HCSB
The Lord God is a sun and shield.
The Lord gives grace and glory.

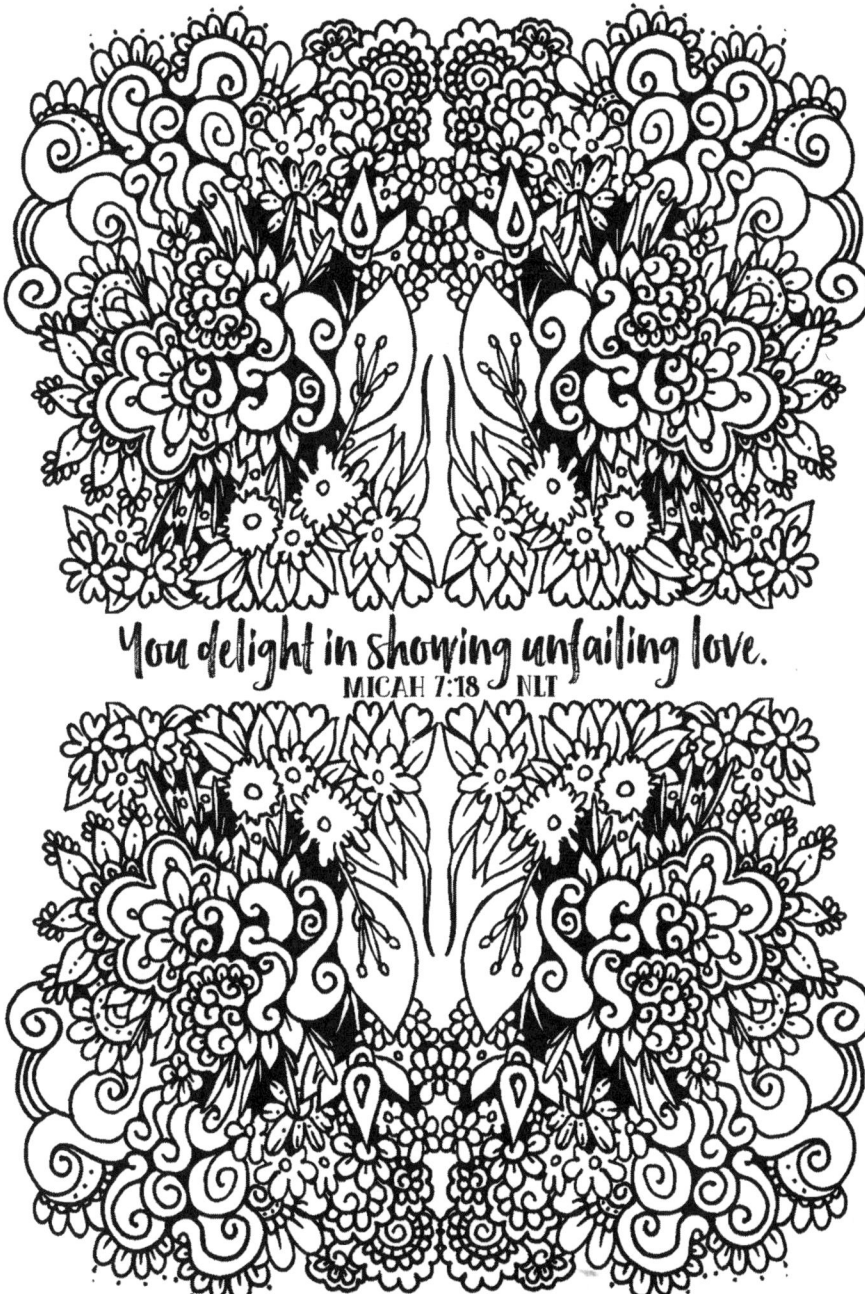
You delight in showing unfailing love.
MICAH 7:18 NLT

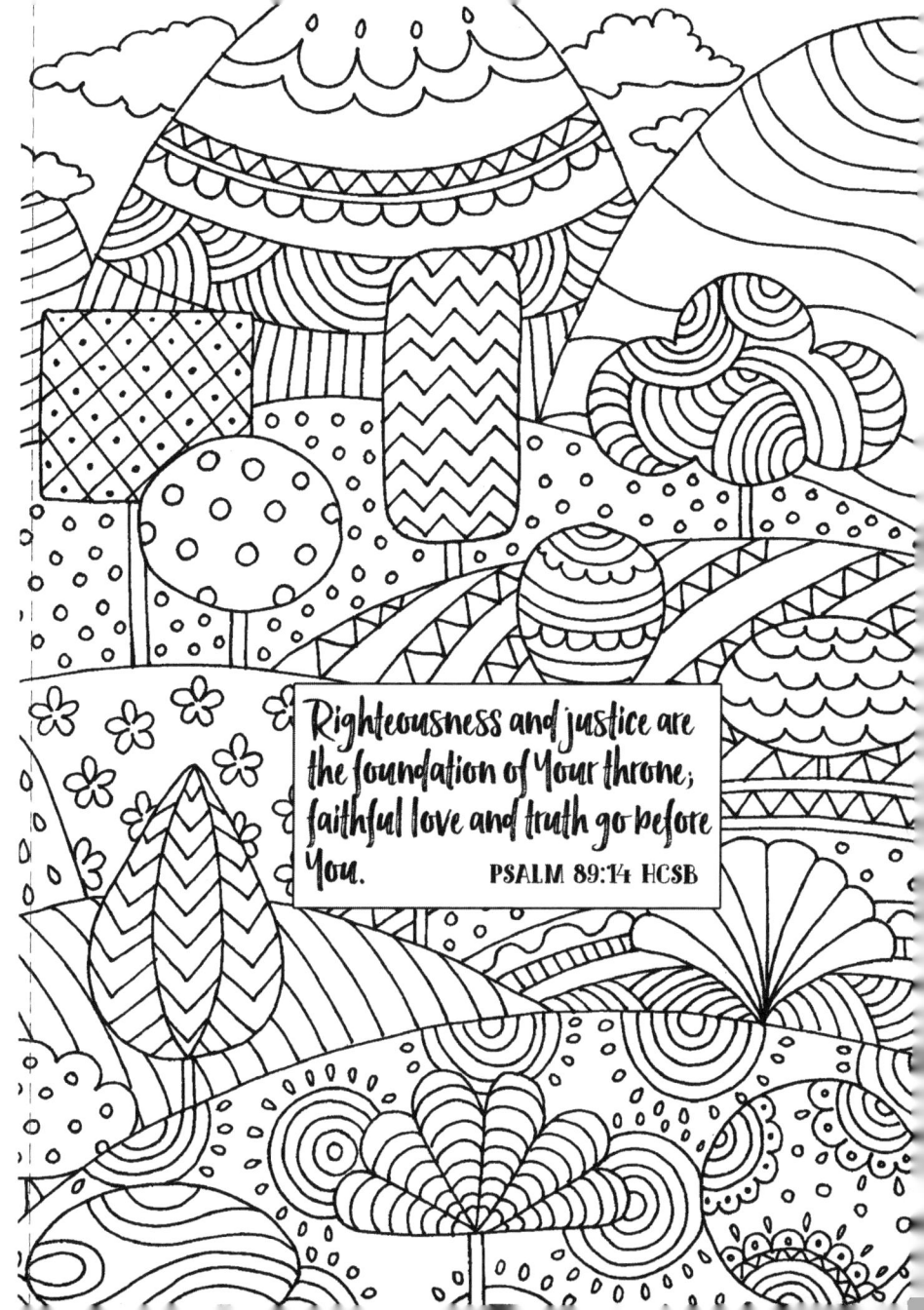
Righteousness and justice are the foundation of Your throne; faithful love and truth go before You.
PSALM 89:14 HCSB

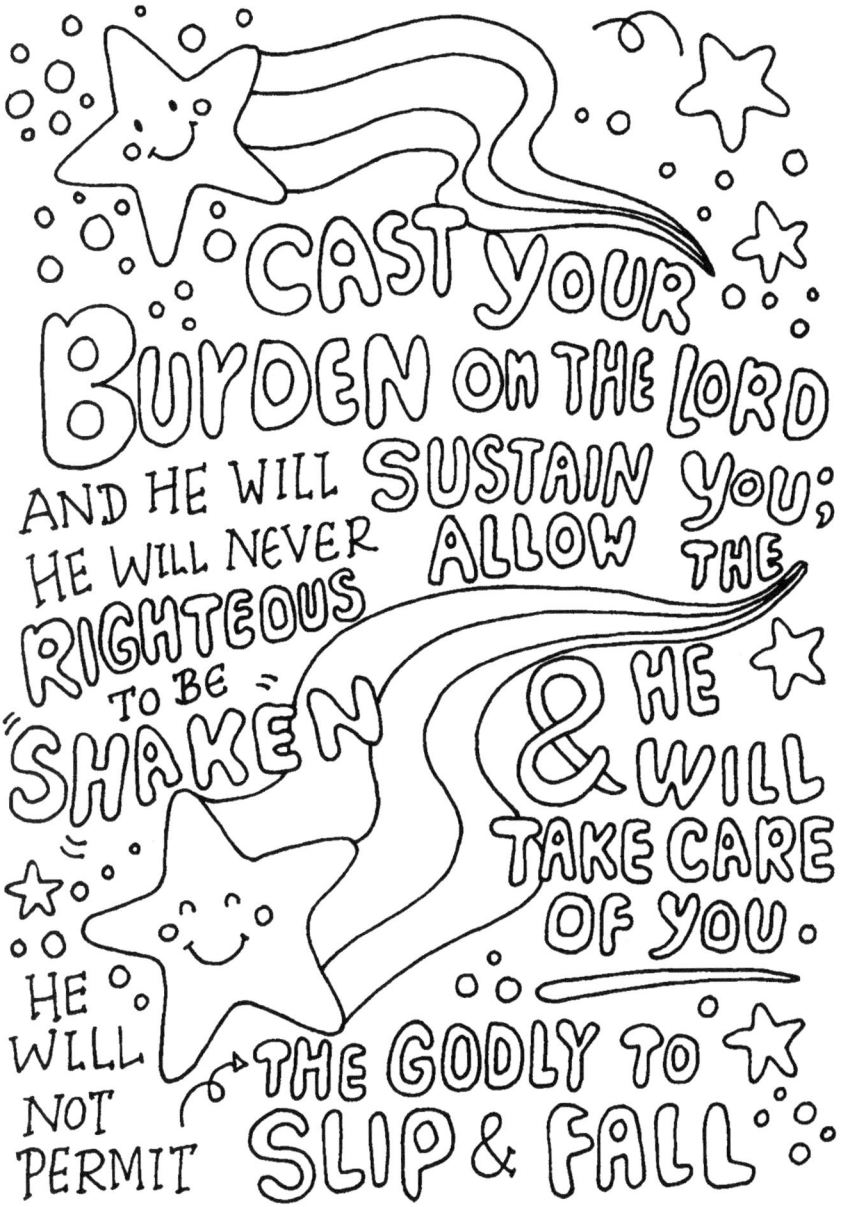

PSALM 55:22 HCSB

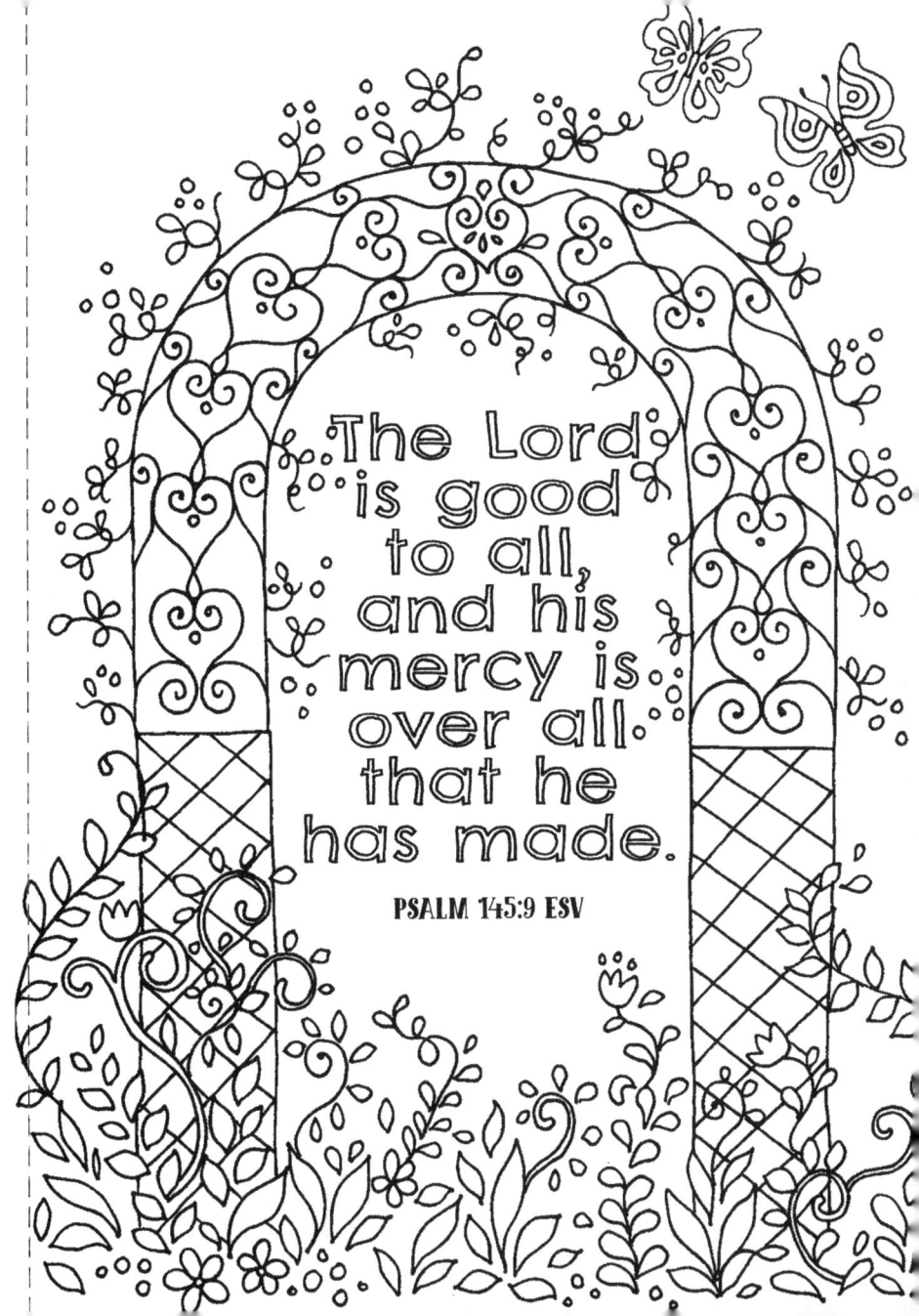
The Lord is good to all, and his mercy is over all that he has made.
PSALM 145:9 ESV

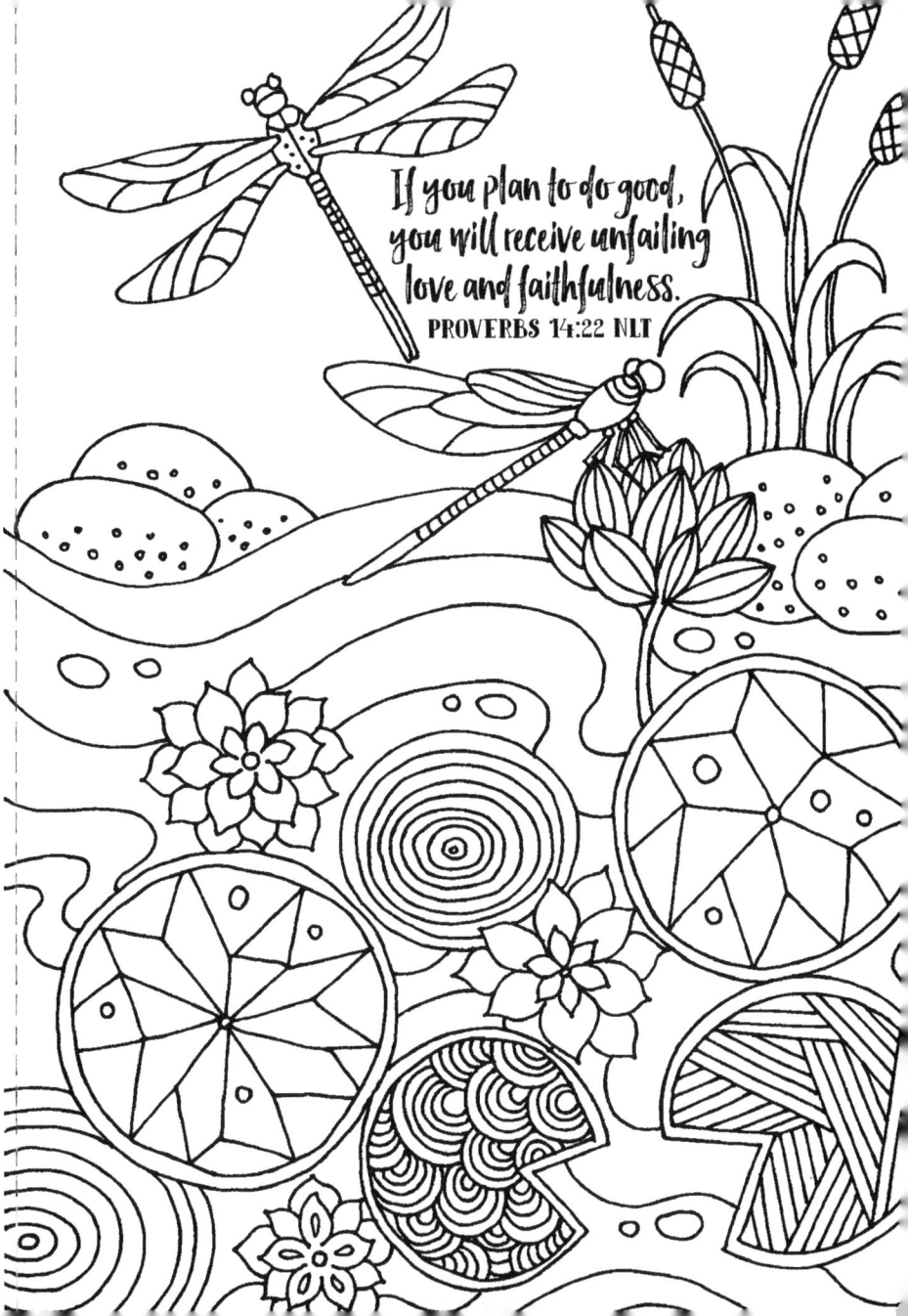
If you plan to do good,
you will receive unfailing
love and faithfulness.
PROVERBS 14:22 NLT

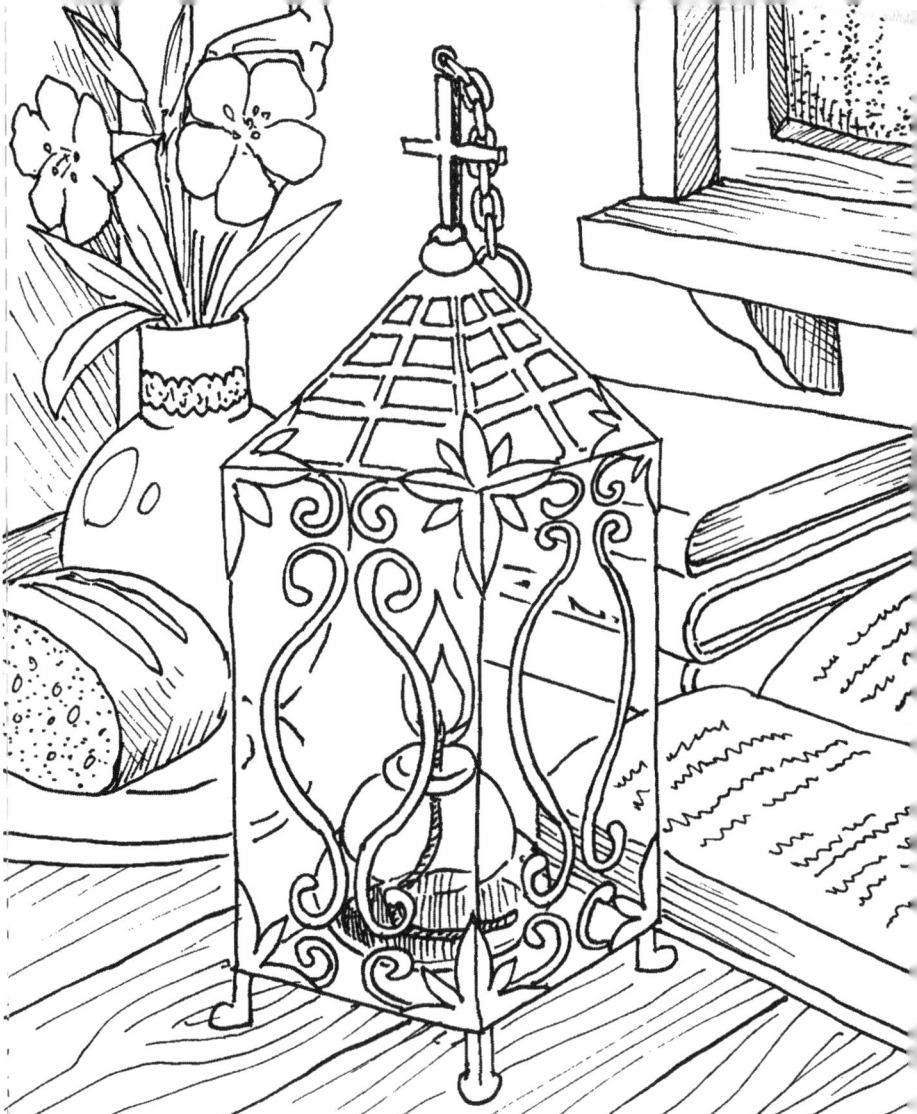

You, Lord, are my lamp;
the Lord turns my darkness into light.

2 SAMUEL 22:29 NIV

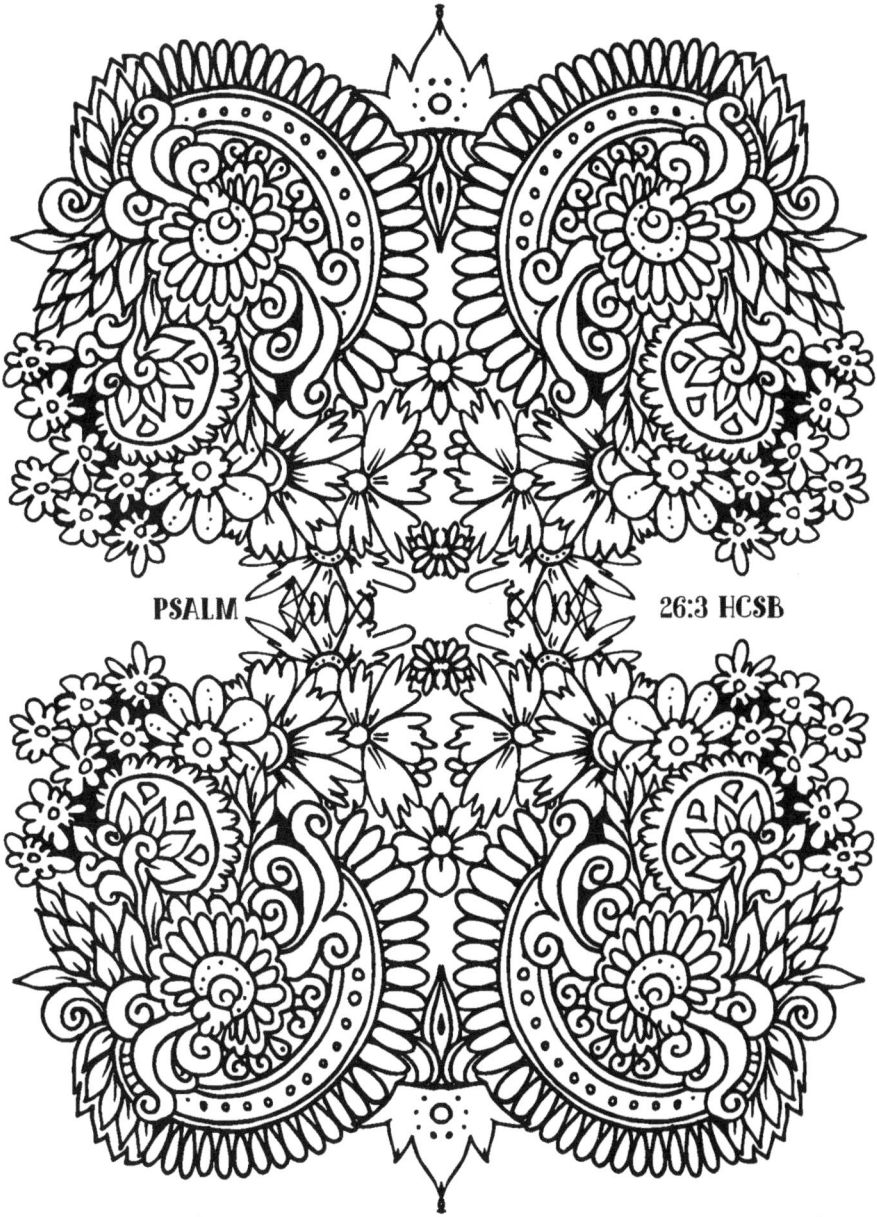

Your faithful love is before my eyes, and I live by Your truth.

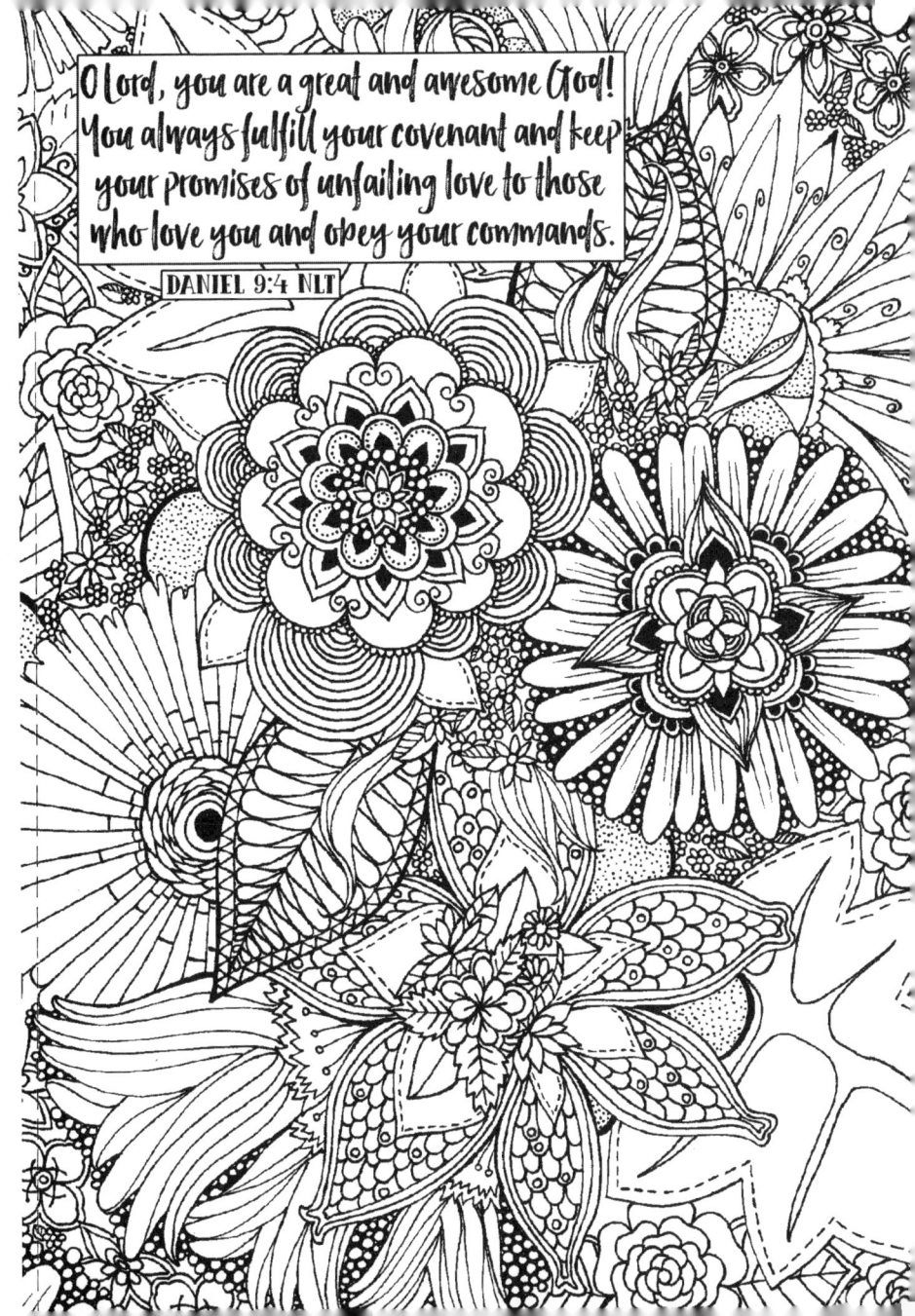
O Lord, you are a great and awesome God!
You always fulfill your covenant and keep
your promises of unfailing love to those
who love you and obey your commands.
DANIEL 9:4 NLT

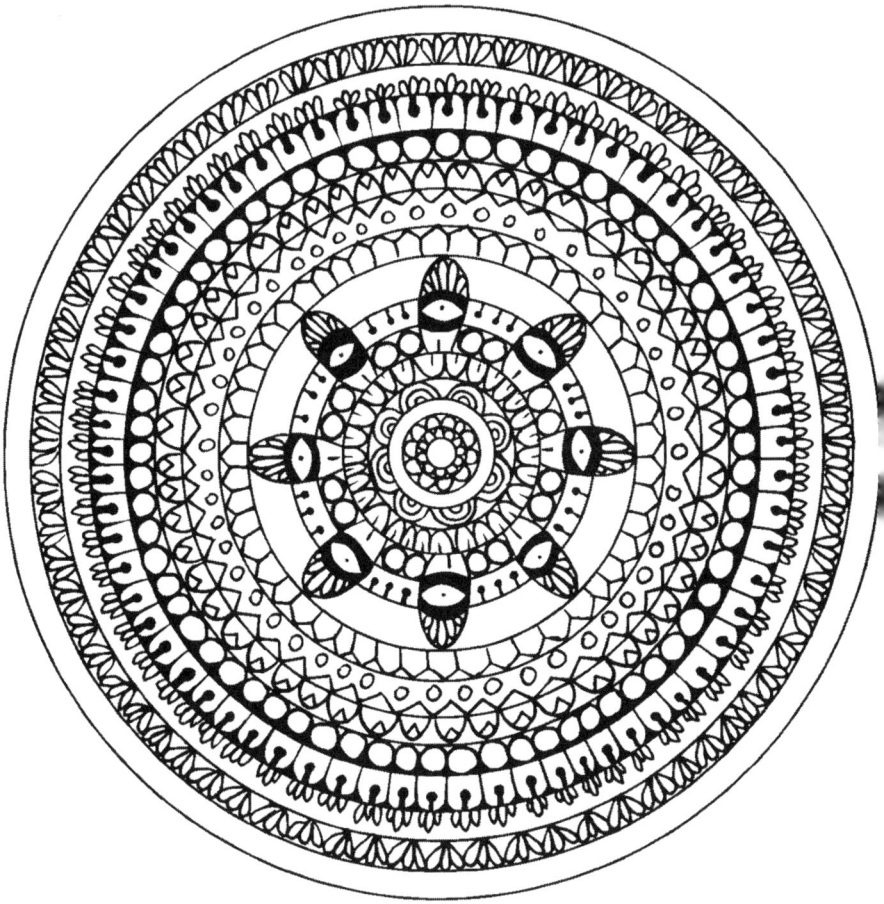

PSALM 145:17 NIV

THE LORD IS RIGHTEOUS
IN ALL HIS WAYS AND
FAITHFUL IN ALL HE DOES.

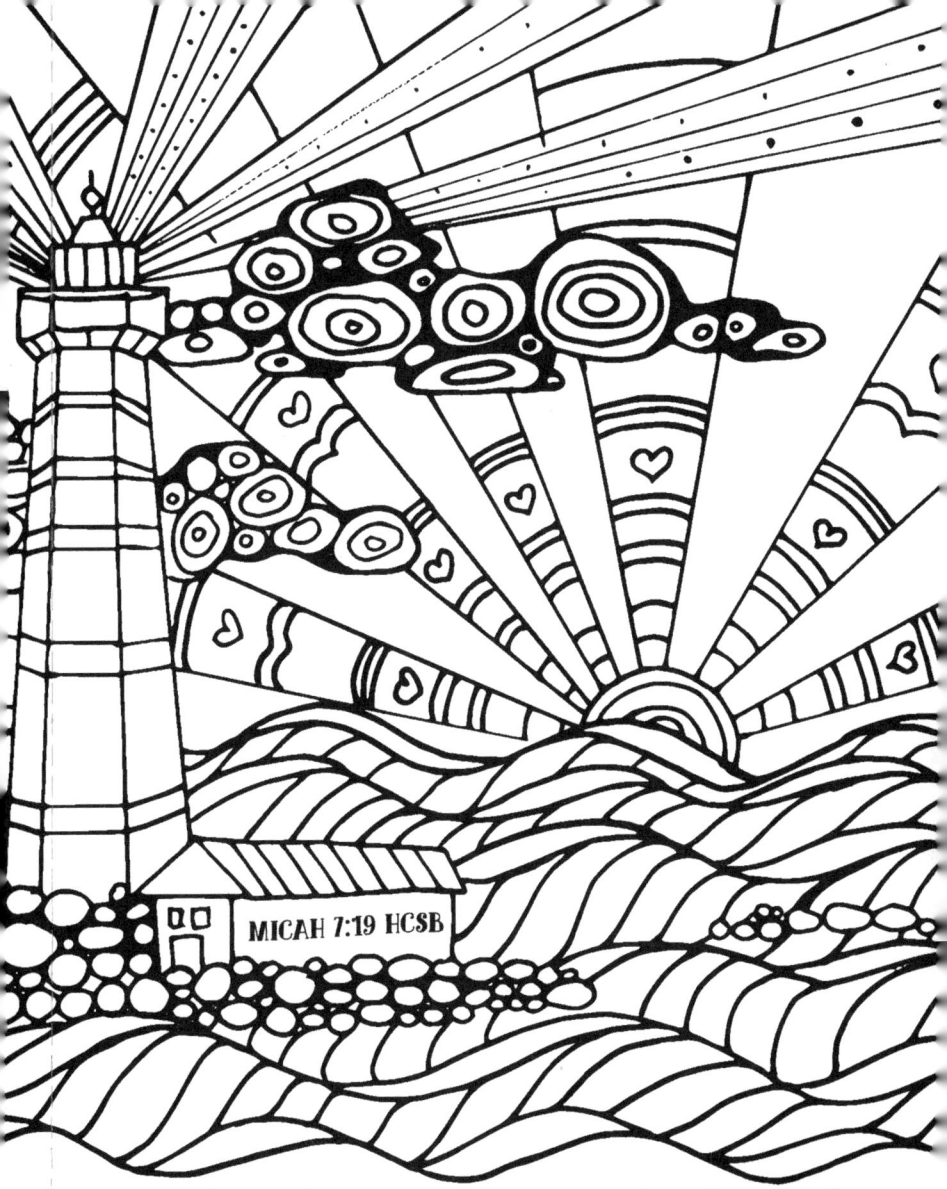

He will again have compassion on us; He will vanquish our iniquities. You will cast all our sins into the depths of the sea.

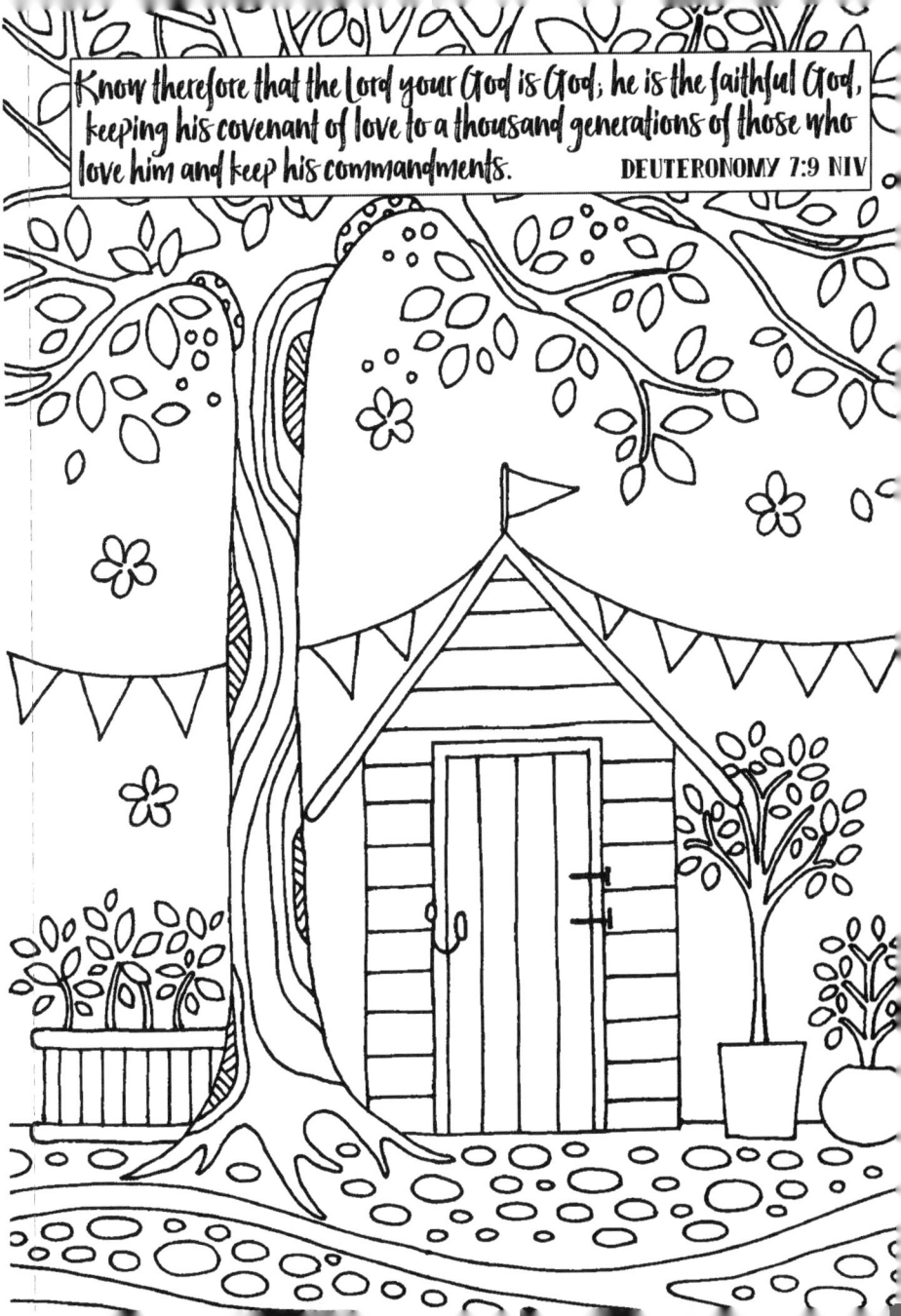
Know therefore that the Lord your God is God; he is the faithful God, keeping his covenant of love to a thousand generations of those who love him and keep his commandments.
DEUTERONOMY 7:9 NIV

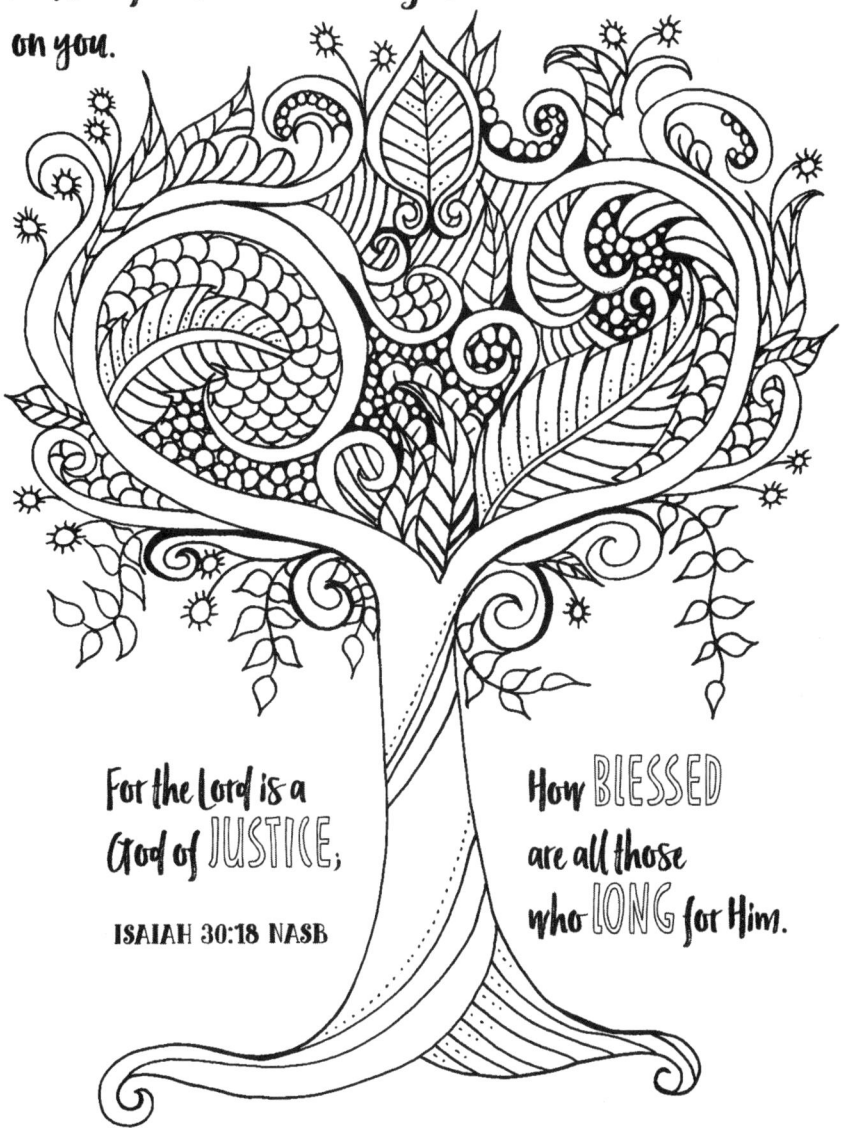
The Lord longs to be GRACIOUS to you,
And therefore He WAITS on high to have COMPASSION
on you.
For the Lord is a
God of JUSTICE;
ISAIAH 30:18 NASB
How BLESSED
are all those
who LONG for Him.

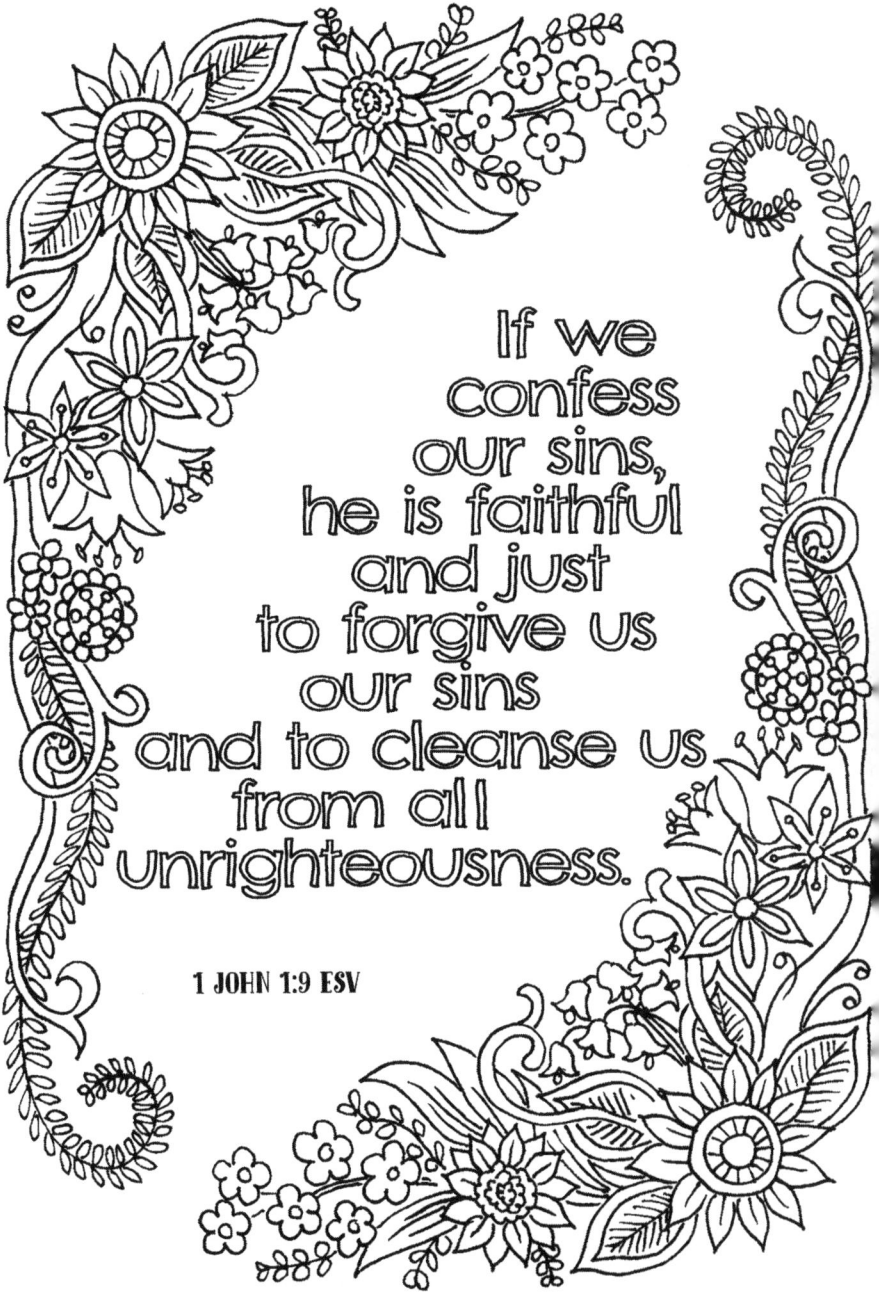
If we
confess
our sins,
he is faithful
and just
to forgive us
our sins
and to cleanse us
from all
unrighteousness.
1 JOHN 1:9 ESV

FOR YOU ARE SAVED BY GRACE THROUGH FAITH,
AND THIS IS NOT FROM YOURSELVES;
IT IS GOD'S GIFT

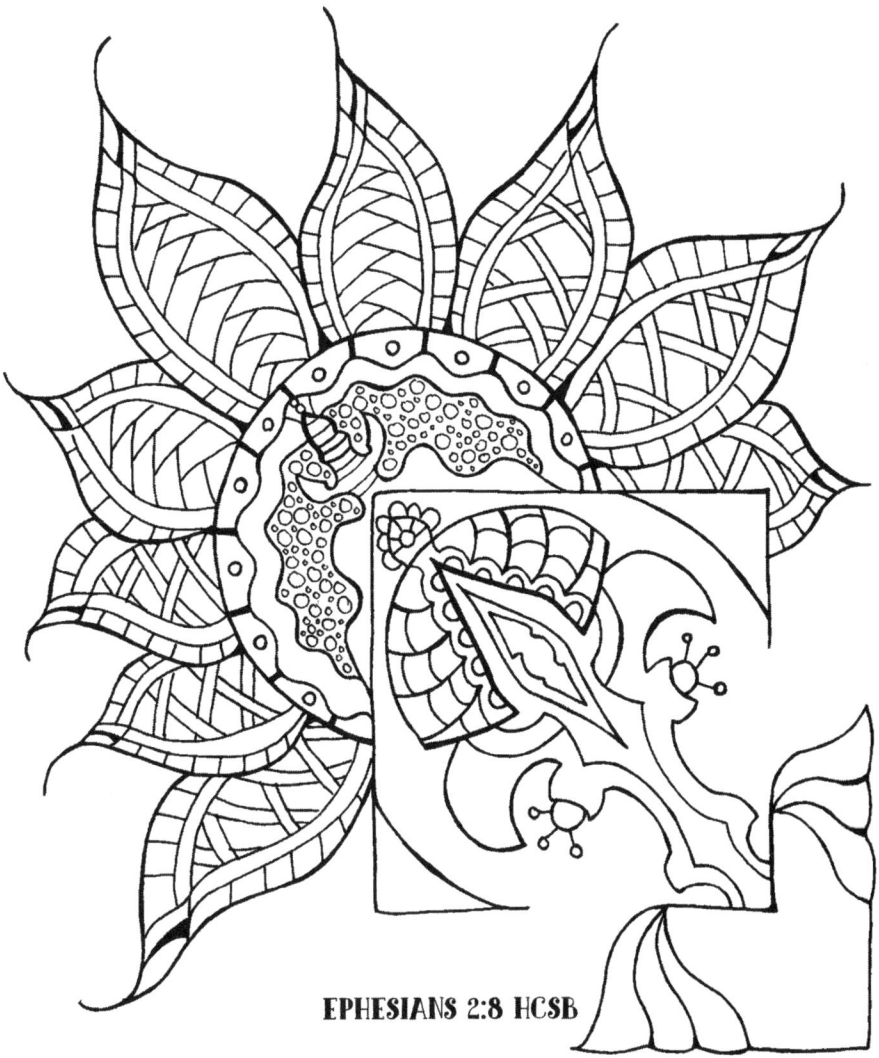

EPHESIANS 2:8 HCSB

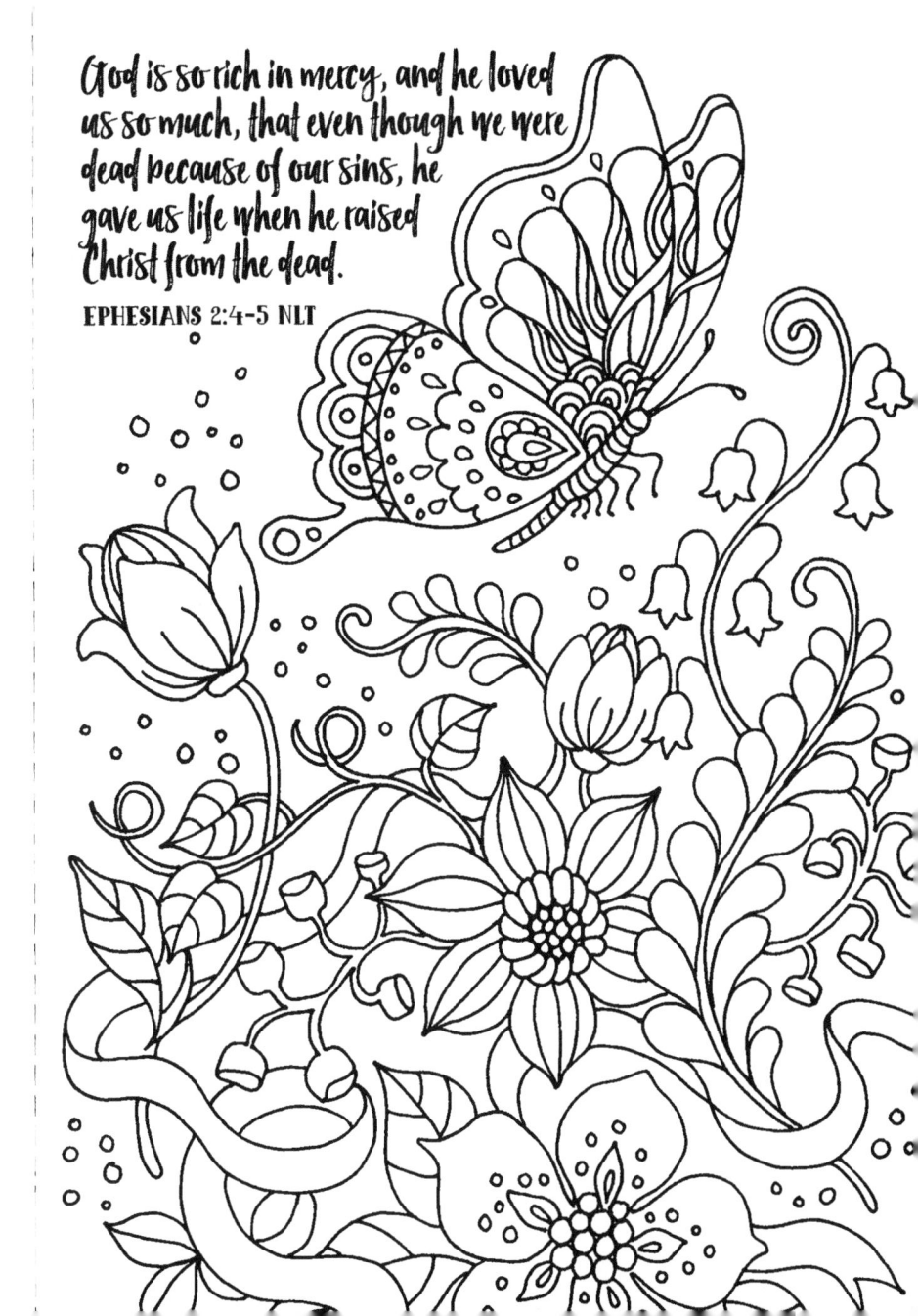
God is so rich in mercy, and he loved us so much, that even though we were dead because of our sins, he gave us life when he raised Christ from the dead.
EPHESIANS 2:4-5 NLT

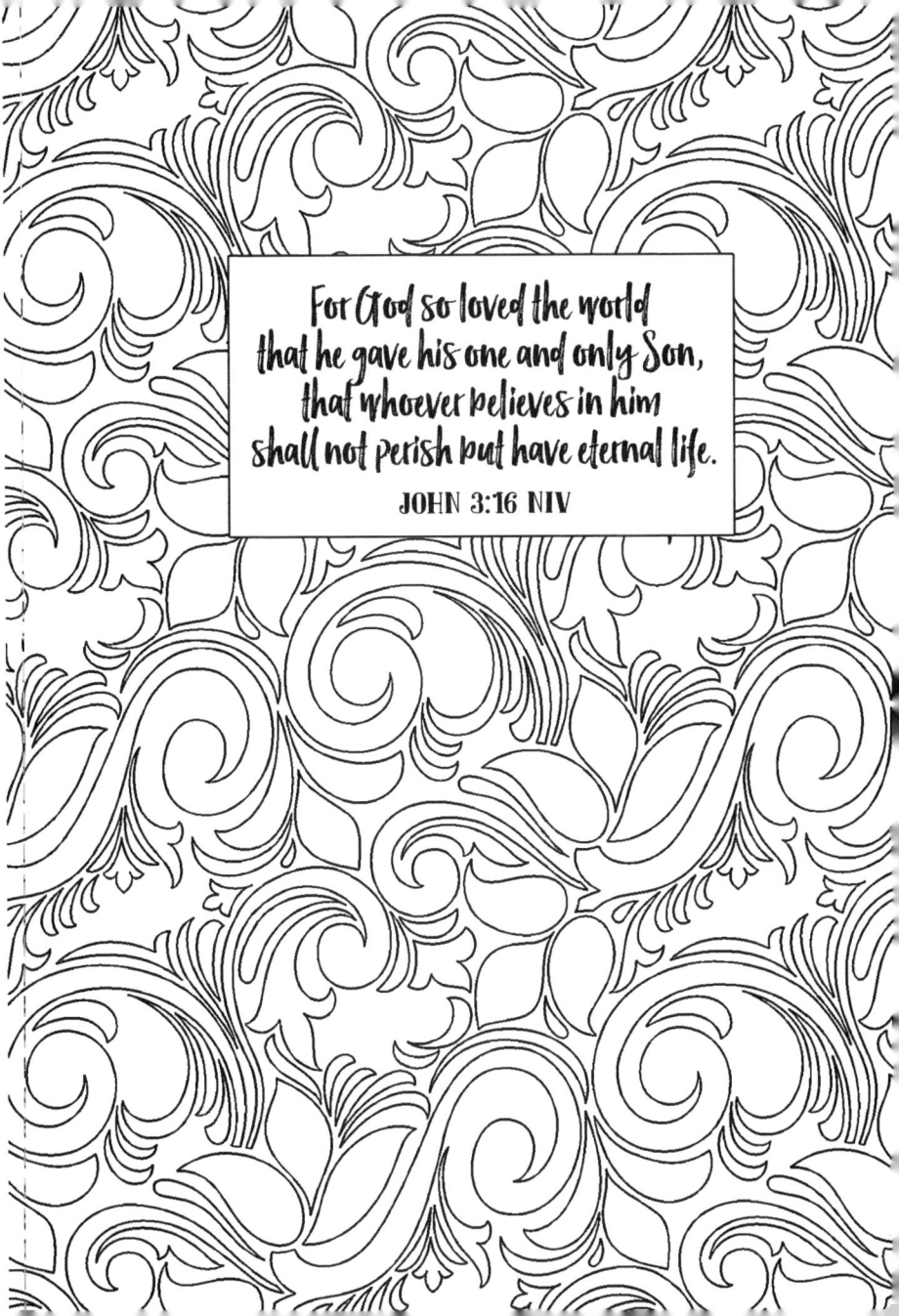
For God so loved the world
that he gave his one and only Son,
that whoever believes in him
shall not perish but have eternal life.
JOHN 3:16 NIV

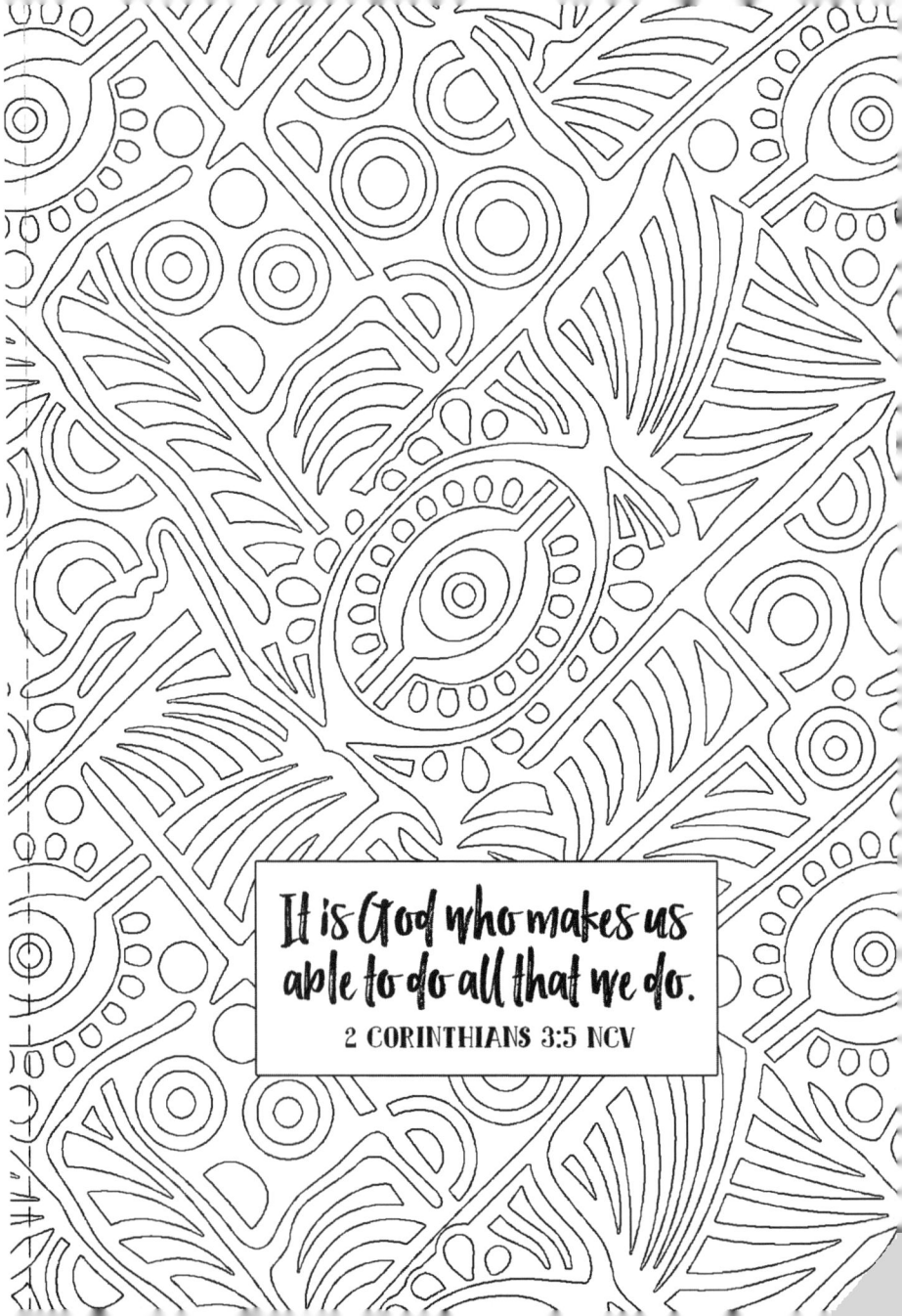
It is God who makes us
able to do all that we do.
2 CORINTHIANS 3:5 NCV

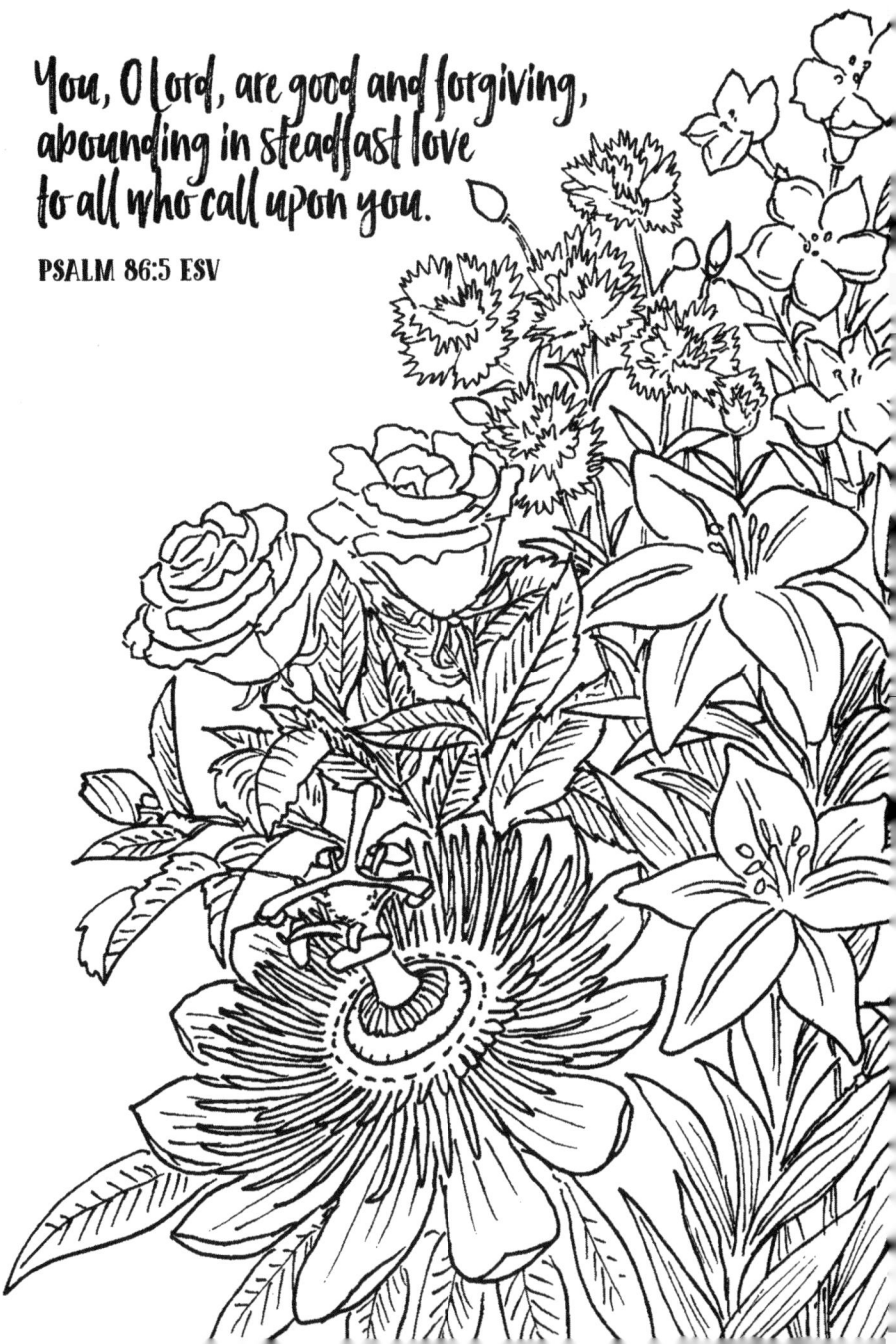
You, O Lord, are good and forgiving,
abounding in steadfast love
to all who call upon you.
PSALM 86:5 ESV

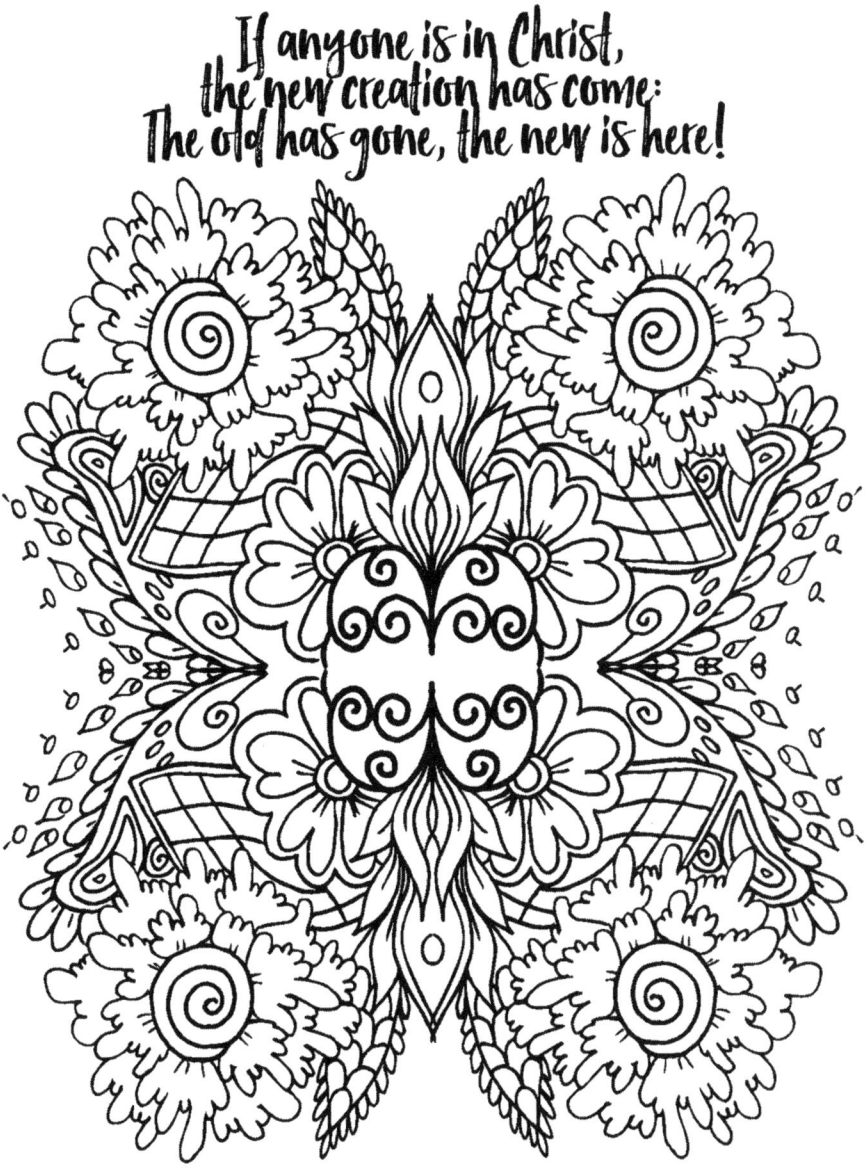

2 CORINTHIANS 5:17 NIV

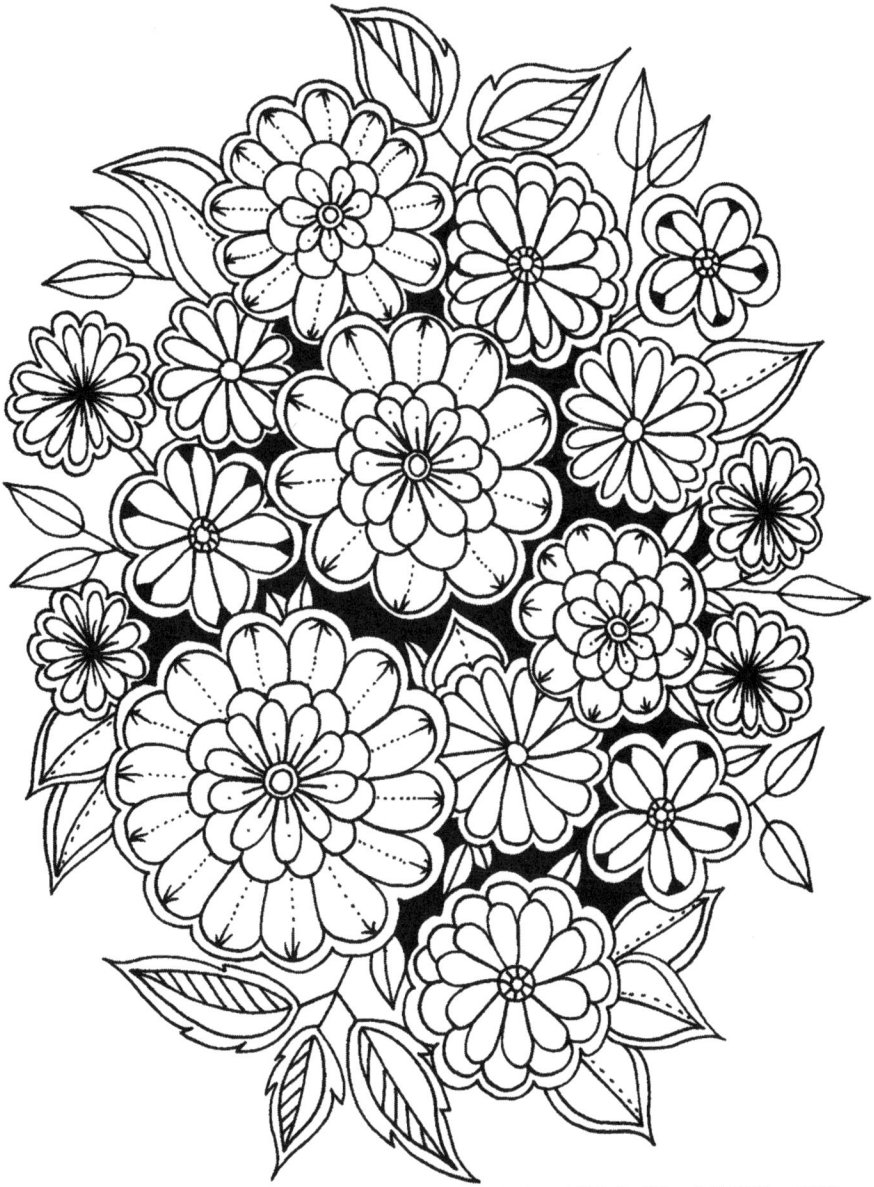

THE LORD IS MERCIFUL AND GRACIOUS; SLOW TO ANGER AND ABOUNDING IN STEADFAST LOVE.

PSALM 103:8 NRSV

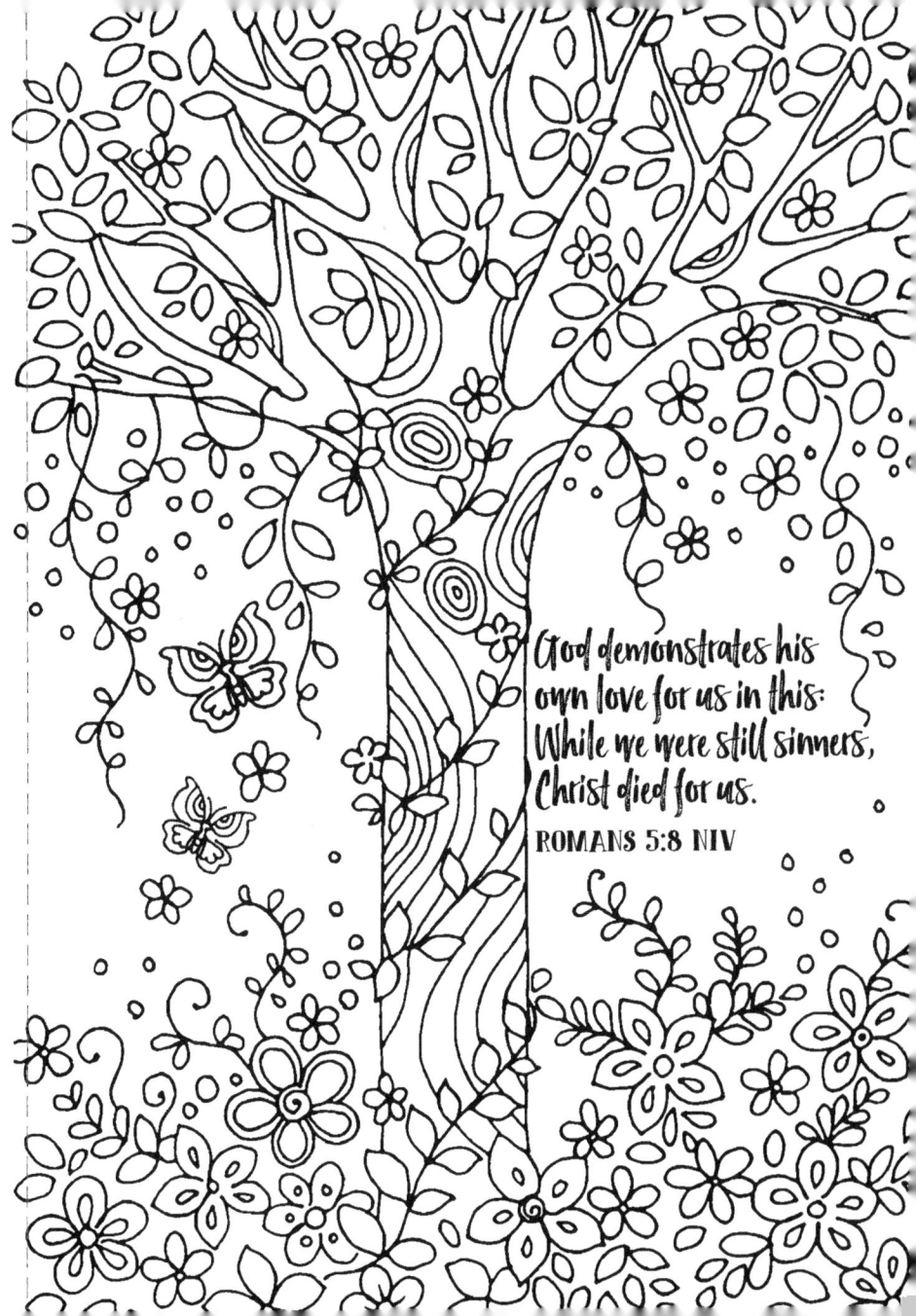
God demonstrates his
own love for us in this:
While we were still sinners,
Christ died for us.
ROMANS 5:8 NIV

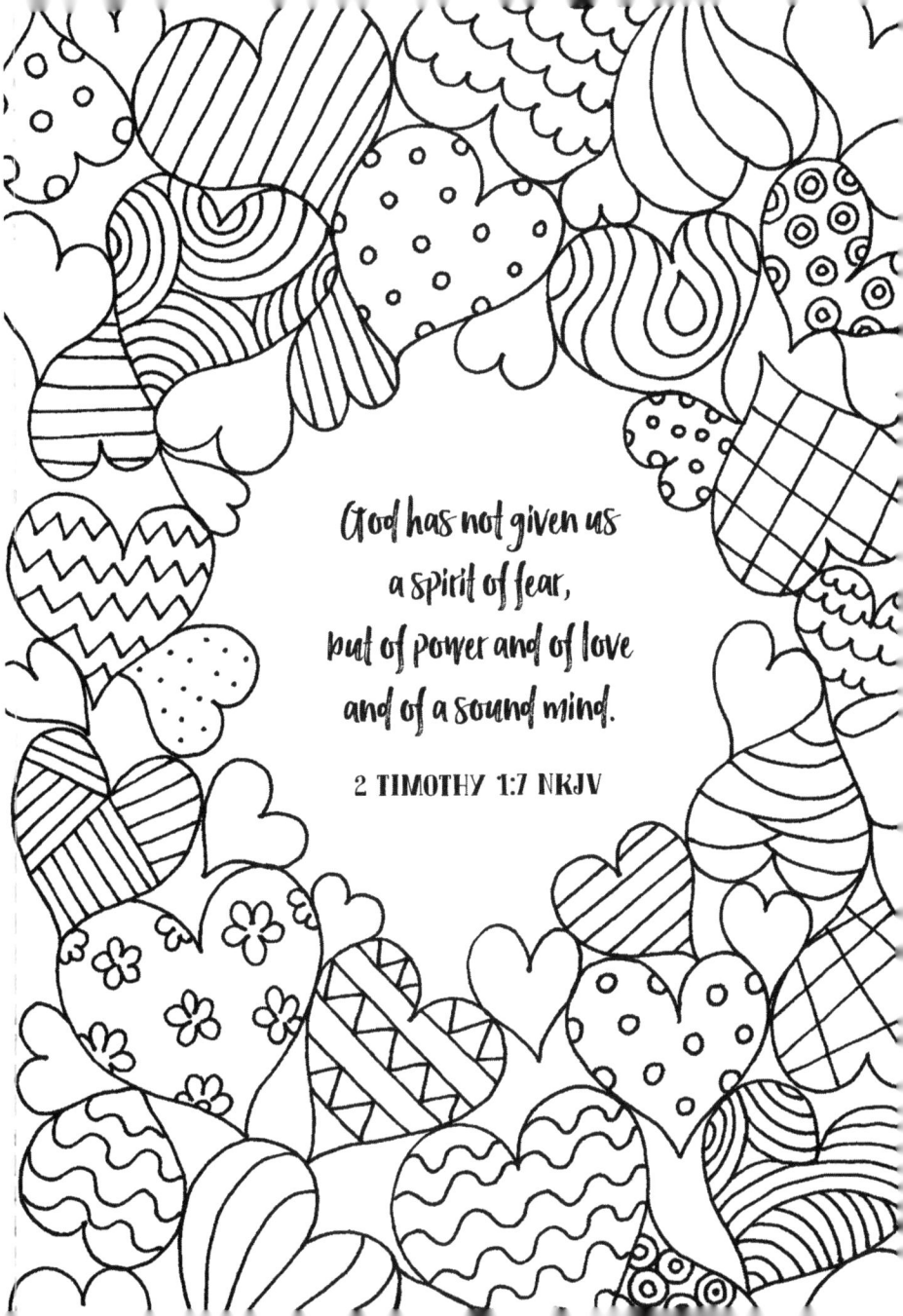
God has not given us
a spirit of fear,
but of power and of love
and of a sound mind.
2 TIMOTHY 1:7 NKJV

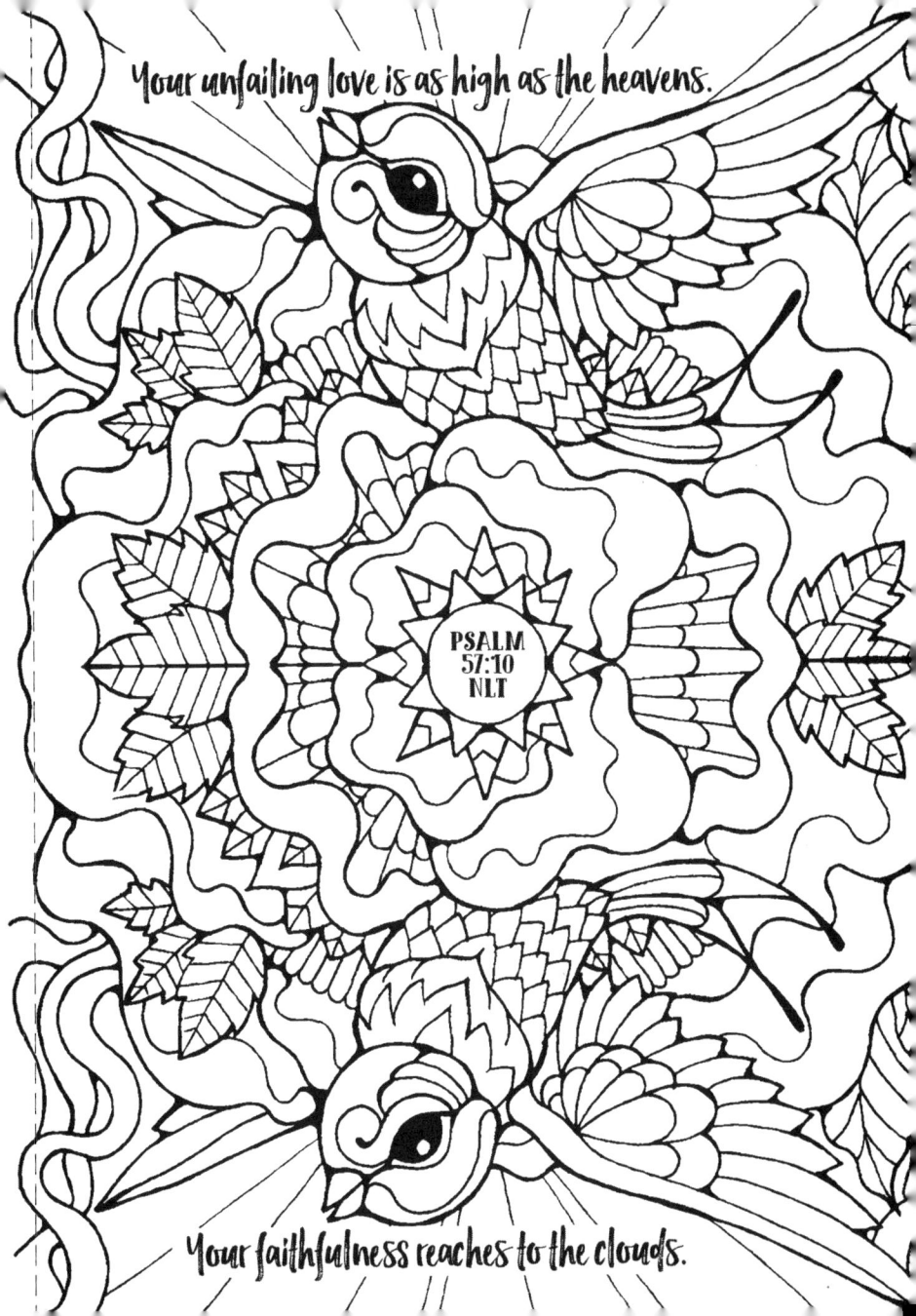
Your unfailing love is as high as the heavens.
PSALM
57:10
NLT
Your faithfulness reaches to the clouds.

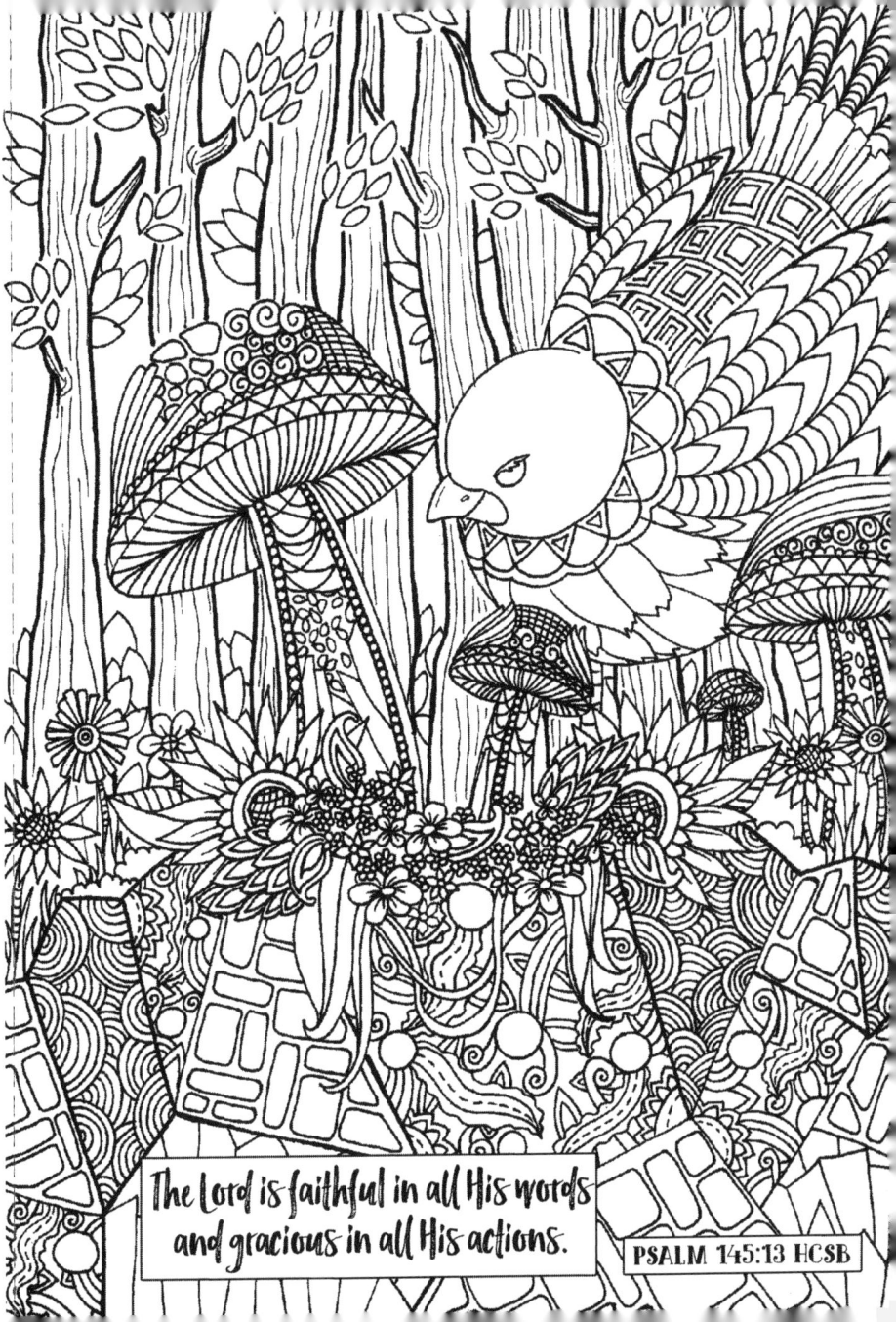
The Lord is faithful in all His words
and gracious in all His actions.
PSALM 145:13 HCSB

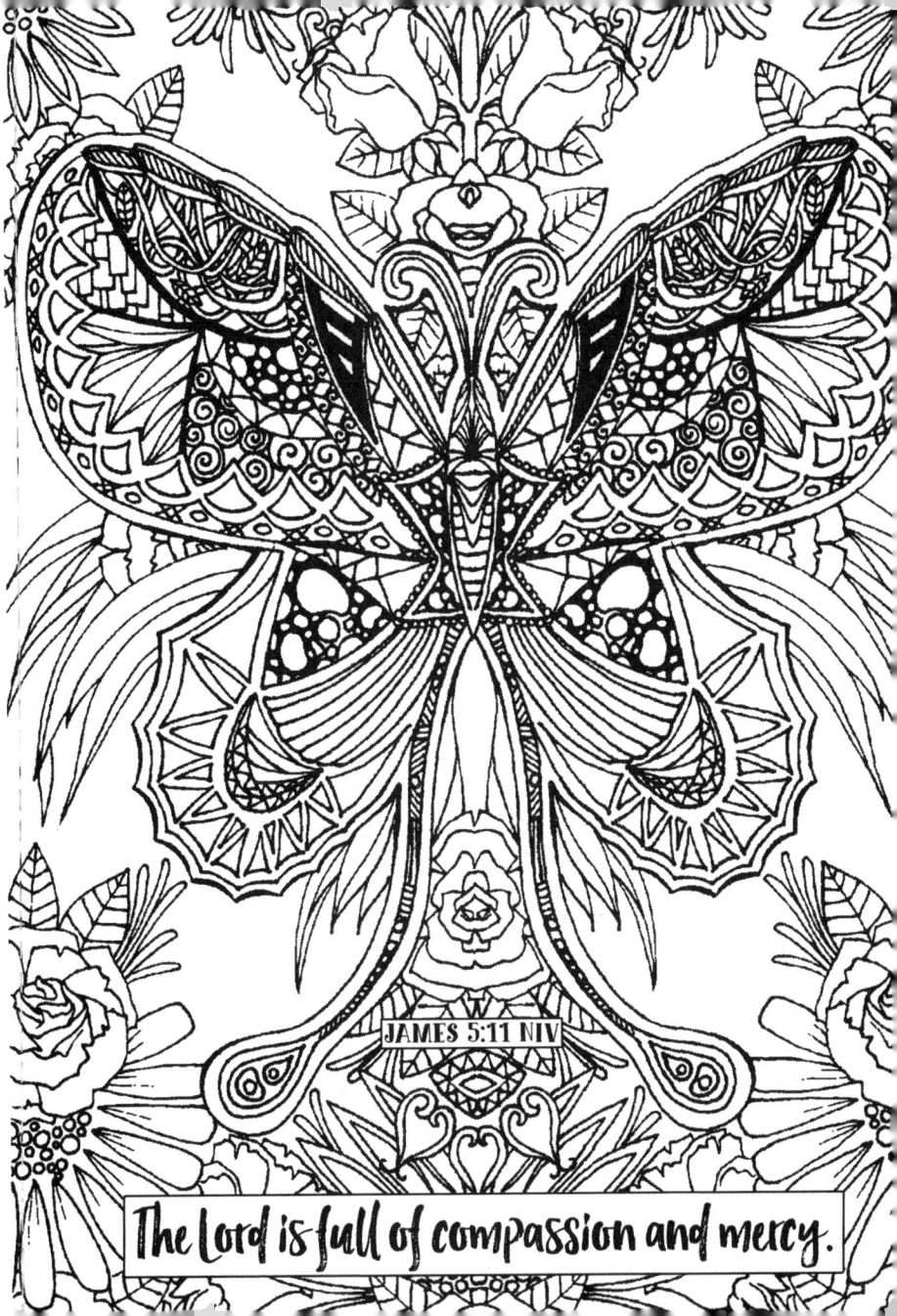
JAMES 5:11 NIV
The Lord is full of compassion and mercy.

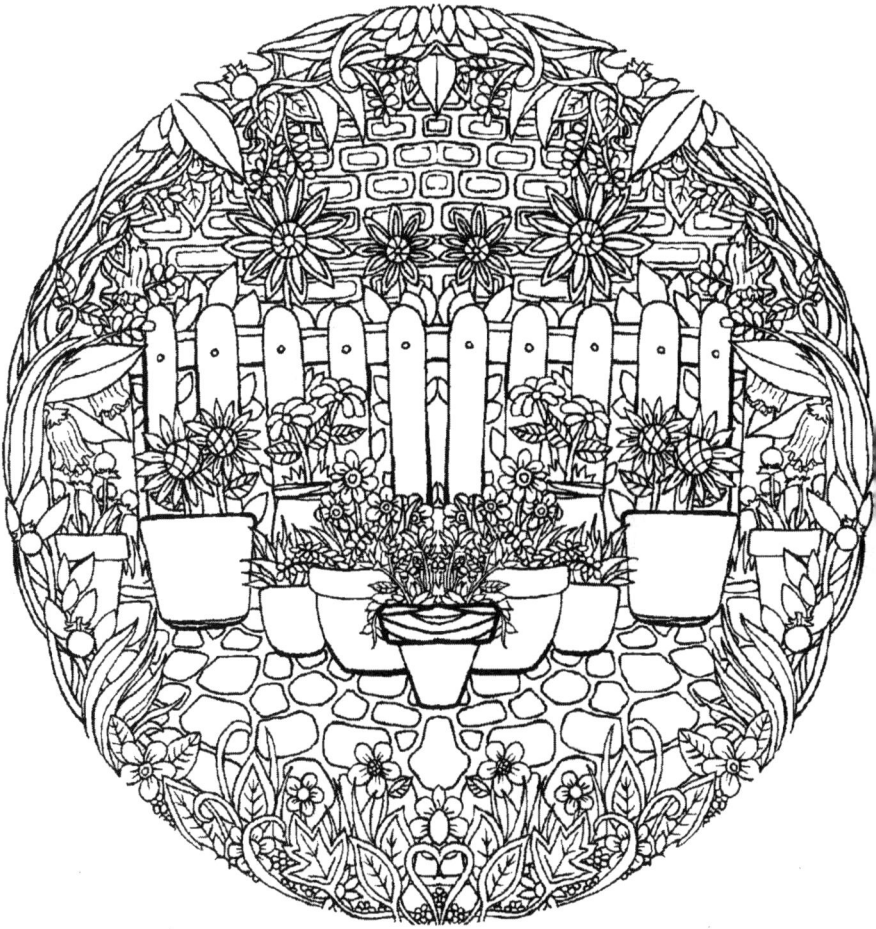

FOR THE LORD IS GOOD;
HIS STEADFAST LOVE ENDURES FOREVER,
AND HIS FAITHFULNESS TO ALL GENERATIONS.

PSALM 100:5 ESV

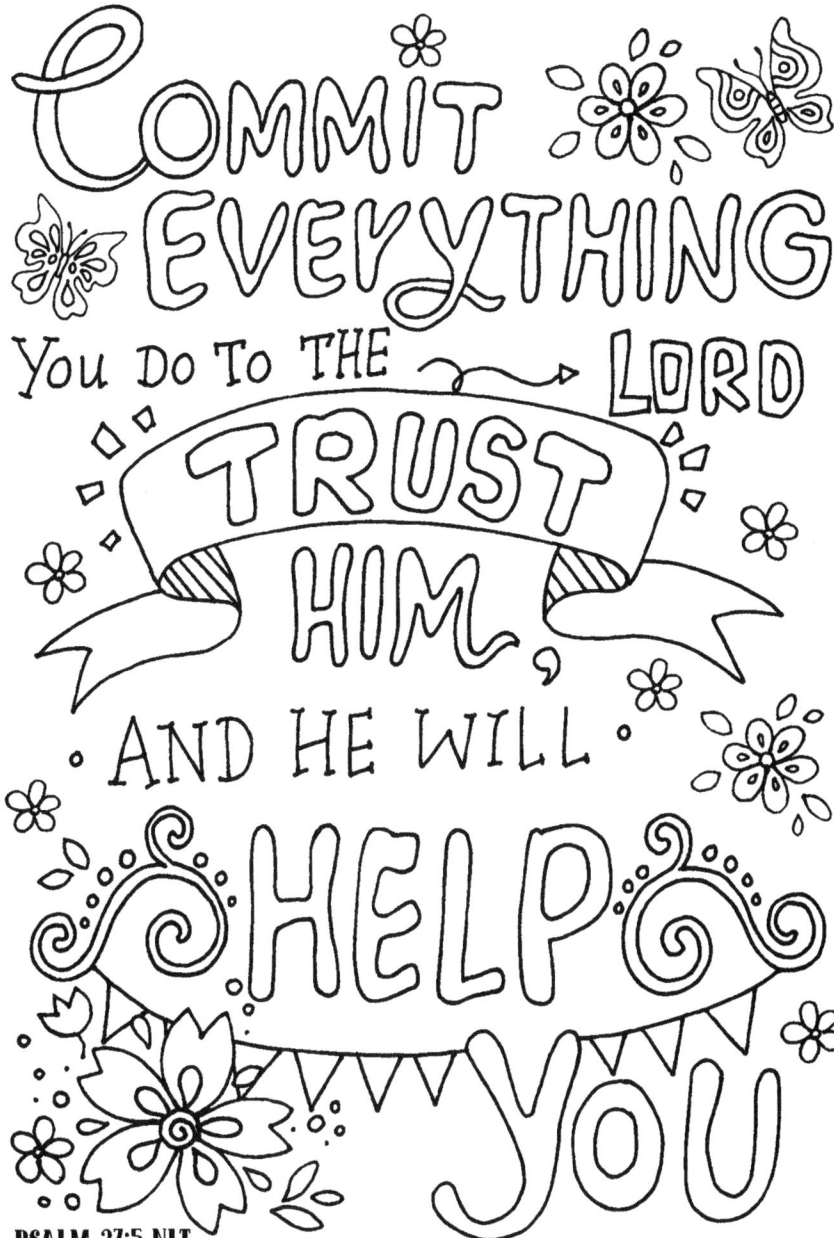
COMMIT EVERYTHING
YOU DO TO THE LORD
TRUST HIM,
AND HE WILL
HELP YOU
PSALM 37:5 NLT

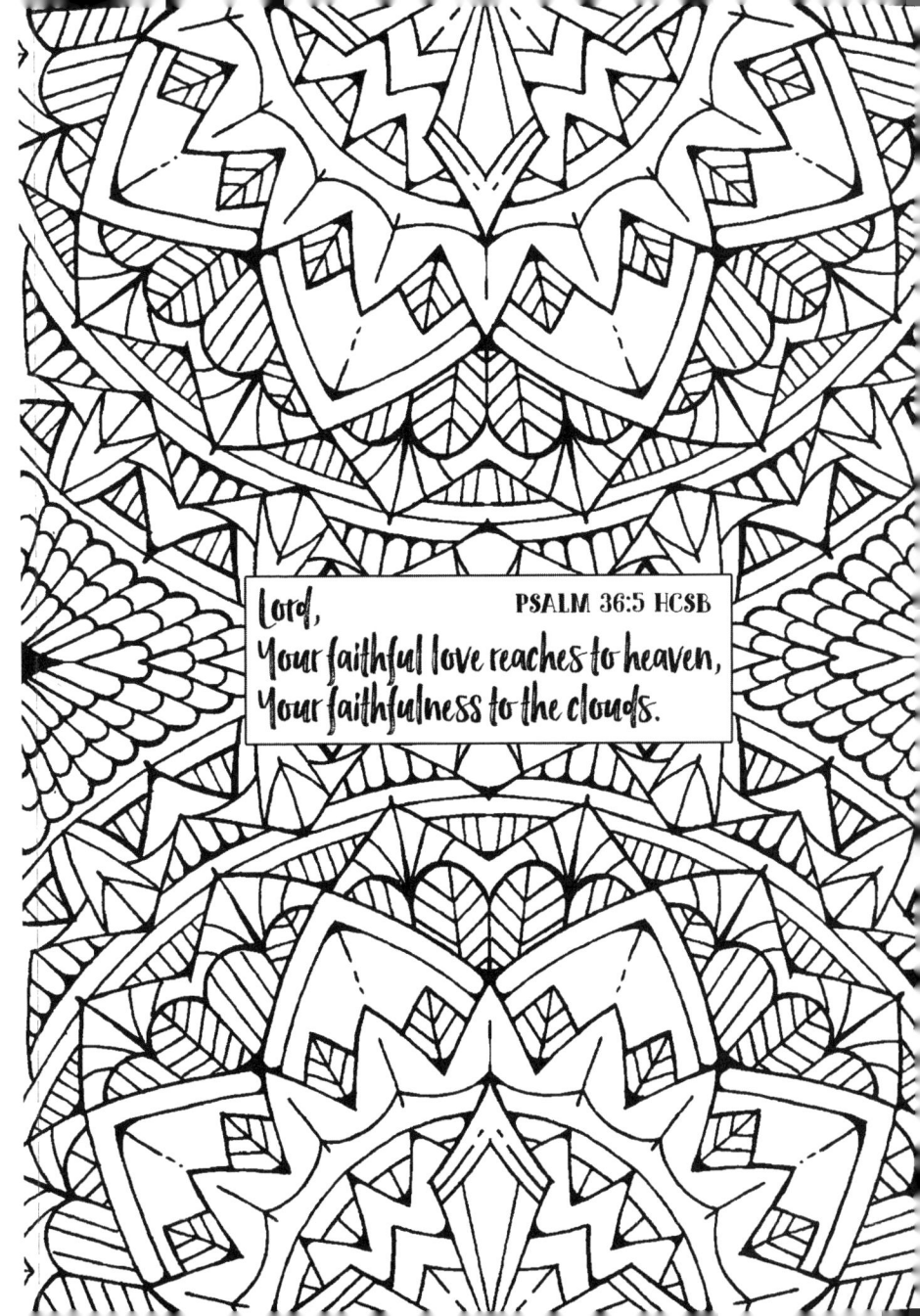
Lord,
PSALM 36:5 HCSB
Your faithful love reaches to heaven,
Your faithfulness to the clouds.

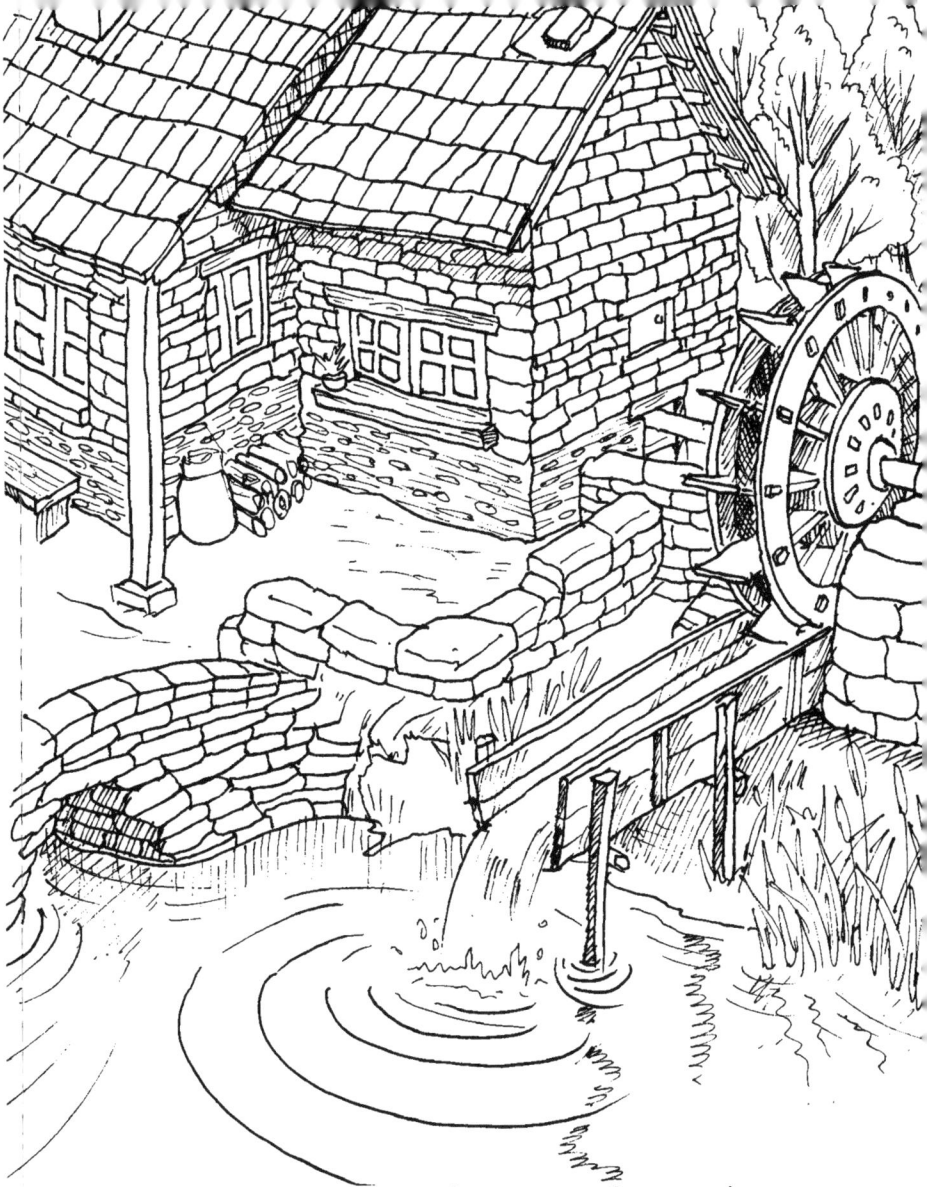

The end of all things is at hand; therefore be self-controlled and sober-minded for the sake of your prayers. **1 PETER 4:7 ESV**

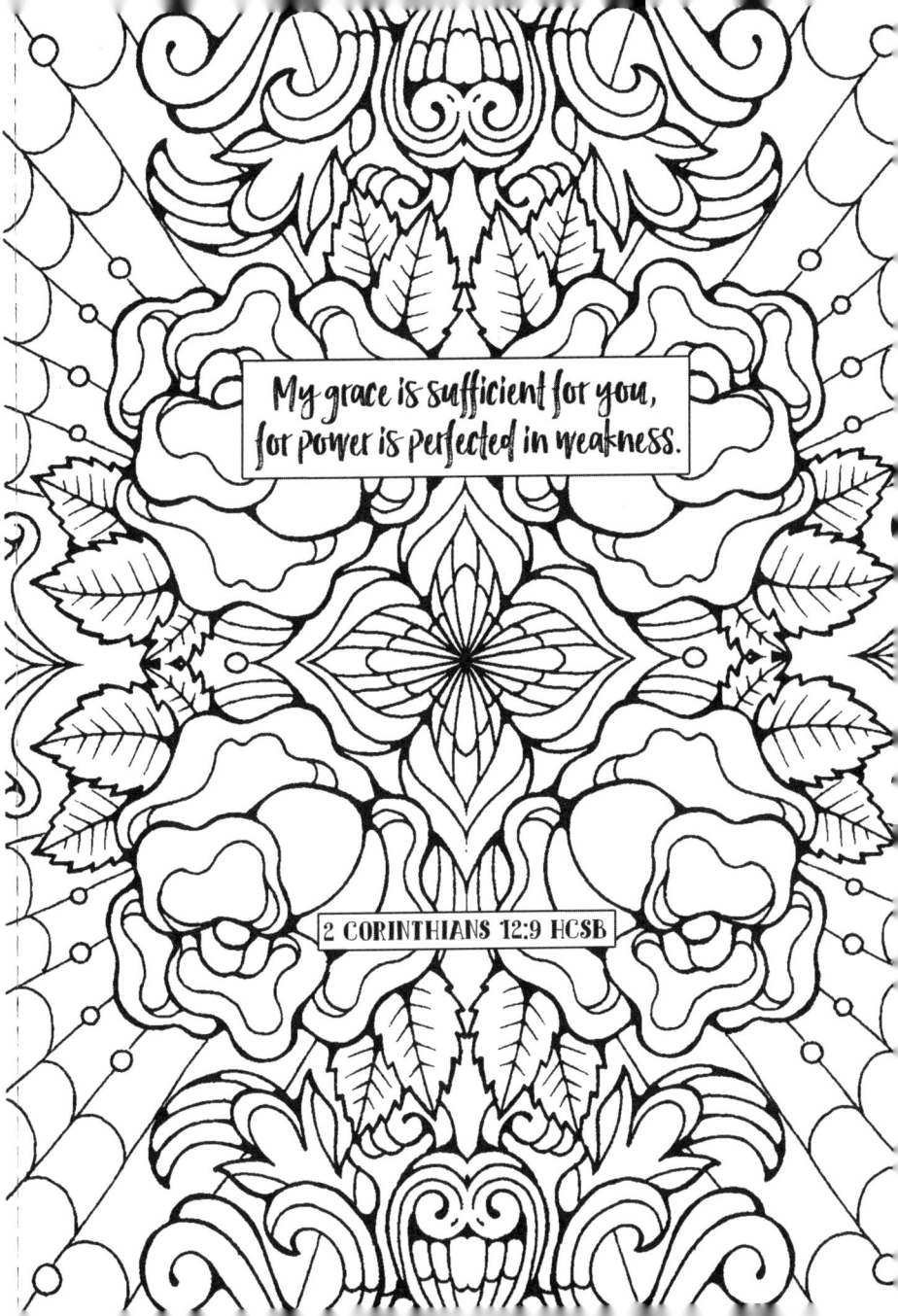
My grace is sufficient for you,
for power is perfected in weakness.
2 CORINTHIANS 12:9 HCSB

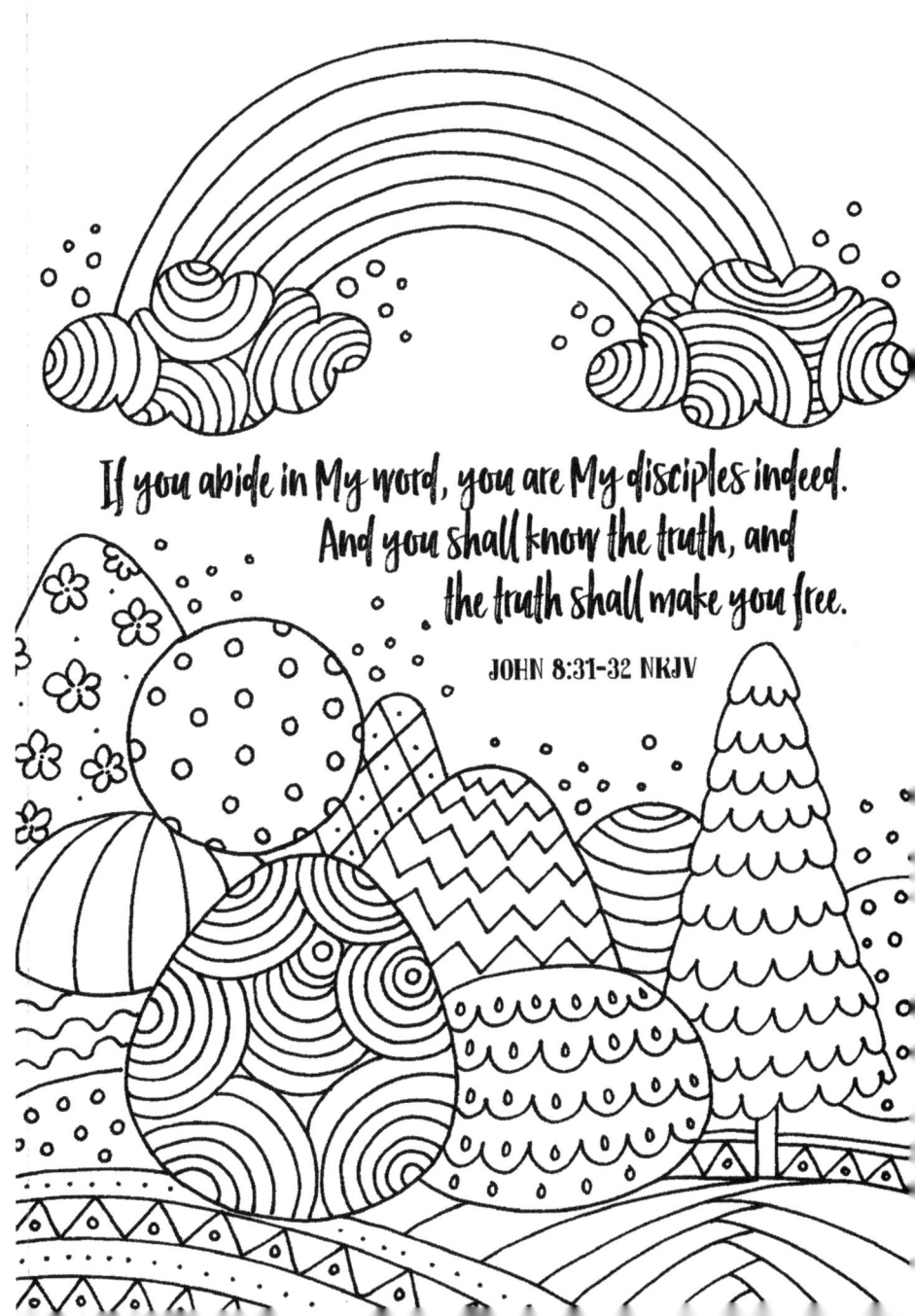
If you abide in My word, you are My disciples indeed.
And you shall know the truth, and
the truth shall make you free.
JOHN 8:31-32 NKJV

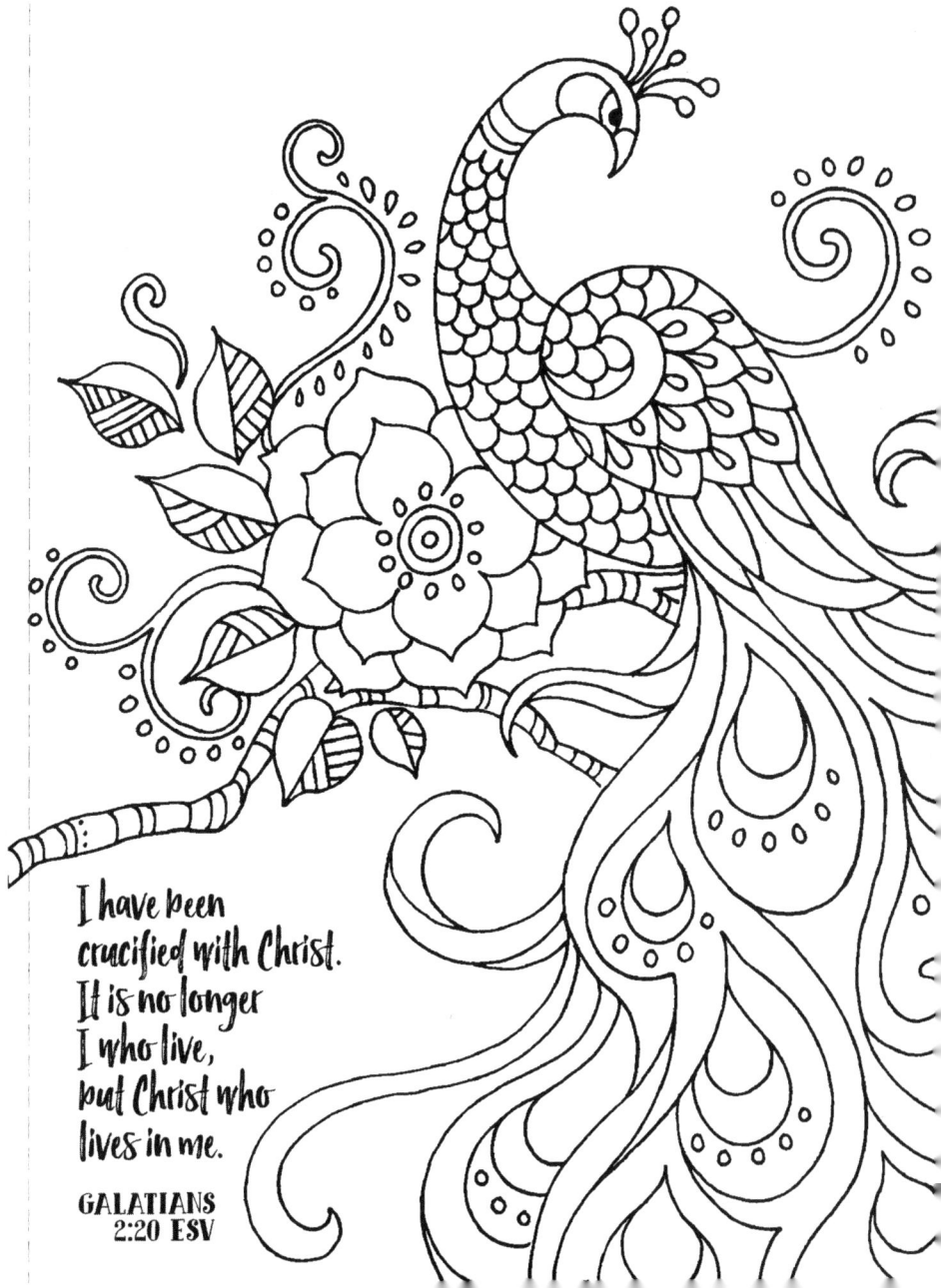
I have been
crucified with Christ.
It is no longer
I who live,
but Christ who
lives in me.
GALATIANS
2:20 ESV